GRAND MOTHERS

Poems, Reminiscences, and
Short Stories About the Keepers
of Our Traditions

Edited by

Nikki Giovanni

Henry Holt and Company • New York

Henry Holt and Company, Inc.
Publishers since 1866
115 West 18th Street
New York, New York 10011

Henry Holt is a registered
trademark of Henry Holt and Company, Inc.

Published in Canada by Fitzhenry & Whiteside Ltd.,
195 Allstate Parkway, Markham, Ontario L3R 4T8.

Library of Congress Cataloging-in-Publication Data
Grand mothers: poems, reminiscences, and short stories about the
keepers of our traditions / edited by Nikki Giovanni.
p.   cm.
Summary: Such women as Gwendolyn Brooks, Mary Elizabeth King,
Gloria Naylor, and Kyoko Mori celebrate the unique roles of
grandmothers in nurturing us, preserving our culture, and preparing
us for the future.
1. Grandmothers—Literary collections. [1. Grandmothers—
Literary collections.] I. Giovanni, Nikki. II. Title: Grandmothers.
PZ5.G6955 1994   810.8'03520432—dc20   94-6144

ISBN 0-8050-2766-1 (hardcover)
3 5 7 9 10 8 6 4
ISBN 0-8050-4903-7 (paperback)
1 3 5 7 9 10 8 6 4 2

First published in hardcover in 1994 by Henry Holt and Company, Inc.
First paperback edition, 1996

Printed in the United States of America
on acid-free paper. ∞

GRAND MOTHERS

To: Martina

From:

Mom & Dad

"All eyes do not see Everything"

To the best of all possible times, the grand times with grand mothers
— N. G.

Contents

INTRODUCTION
Nikki Giovanni

Part One

"*. . . What you talkin' 'bout did I love you?*
Girl, I stayed alive for you."
— *Toni Morrison*

Part Two

"Put Me Down Easy, Janie,
Ah'm a Cracked Plate."
— Zora Neale Hurston

Part Three

*"Over the river and through the woods
To Grandmother's house we go . . ."*
—Lydia Maria Child

Introduction

⟨∕⟩

Nikki Giovanni

My grandmother, Emma Louvenia Watson, was famous in family circles for getting into the bathtub without her soap. This is a woman who helped organize resistance to segregation in Knoxville, Tennessee. This is a woman who stood up to Cass Walker, a very conservative Knoxville businessman. This is a woman who was the indirect cause of the family being in Knoxville, Tennessee, in the first place because she smarted off to some white folk in Albany, Georgia. She could not remember her soap.

She could remember how to make miniature Parker House rolls so light that we practically had to put weights on them to keep them on the Sunday table; she made peach or blackberry cobbler so exquisite that we would have eaten it until next year . . . but it wouldn't last that long; she made sherry chicken that fell off the bone; she made her own mayonnaise, which was worth eating on her own homemade bread without any meat at all. But I only mention her food. Grandmother played the piano, could sew like a pro, and would tackle anything foolish enough to bother her children, husband, or mother-in-law. She forgot her soap.

Somehow that bothered this granddaughter when I was

small, but the older I have grown, the more it is a fond memory. Who knows what joy it gave her to sit in a tub of hot water? Maybe she had grown up without indoor plumbing and was just showing off the water in the tub the way she showed off when she scraped the dough from the mixing bowl into the baking pan. We all hated that . . . all four of us. Grandmother would scrape it so clean that there was no reason to ask for the bowl . . . there was nothing to lick. She didn't make the ice cream, Grandpapa did, but she was the one who got to pour. Same results. Nothing in the bowl for four hungry grands. She was opinionated and definite, yet could ask, while she and I watched a television program on world population control, "What does that mean? Abstinence?" She had a strong sense of right and wrong, and she and hers would stand for the right.

Probably the most horrible racial event after the murder of Emmett Till in Money, Mississippi, in 1954 was the murder of the four little girls in Birmingham, Alabama, on September 15, 1963. The girls had gone to Sunday school early to prepare for a special program. Someone had planted a bomb in the church. If Concord fired the shot heard 'round the world, this was the bomb that alerted the world to the fact that something was very wrong in America. The phones started ringing in black communities all over the country, and mass meetings were announced in churches that Sunday. The children, I guess by common consent, were left at home while the adults decided what should be done. Grandmother and Grandpapa went to Mt. Zion Baptist Church early to get a seat up front.

"Nikki," she said to me after coming from the church meeting, "your grandfather and I are too old to march." *I knew something was coming that I would not especially be pleased with.* "But when they asked for volunteers at the meeting tonight"—*what has she promised I will do?*—"I was the first to stand." *Curtains. I'm a goner.* "I told them: John Brown and I are too old to march." *Just get on with it, Grandmother.* "But our granddaughter Nikki is here." *Does my mother know what you are doing?* "And she will march in our place." *My God!* "And everybody applauded." *Sure they did. Those who are about to watch you die salute you.* "Now, John Brown and I will take a cab and come up as soon as the line is in place. You better get on to bed since you have a lot to do tomorrow." Did I mention she hadn't taken her hat off? I did survive that picket line and many others, but her attitude was: Isn't this great? You get to picket! It wasn't often that we said no to her.

One time that I did, however, was when she decided to teach me how to play the piano. My sister, Gary, already played like an angel or whatever heavenly being plays piano. Me, I was a good listener. Grandmother would call us in, William, Terry, Gary, and me, and line us up. We were supposed to do the scales. Gary probably had to play "Clair de Lune" or "Rhapsody in Blue" or some nocturne by Chopin. Me, I couldn't do the scales right. Something about placing your fingers on the right keys and not looking at your hands. Grandmother had one very bad habit: she punished physically. She took a number-two yellow pencil and hit my knuckles. No. A thousand times *no.* I remember saying very calmly to her, "Grandmother, if you are going to be abusive, I am not going to sit here." I proceeded to get up. "Abusive!" she bellowed. "Well, I never." And that was the end of that. She punished me by not teaching me. Abusive, indeed. Recently I was talking about this to my sister, who said, "I didn't realize we could say no to Grandmother." Grandmother never remembered her soap, either.

It was Sweetheart soap: big, oval, and pink. I don't think anything other than perhaps the old blue Sutton Stick deodorant, which Mommy let us use after Gary and I were cleaned up for evening dinner, has smelled as sweet. They don't make Sutton Stick anymore. And I don't use deodorant.

Grandmother did the laundry on Mondays. Every Monday. The trick to the washing was to put your sheets out the night before and sleep on the mattress cover. Otherwise, at the crack of dawn ("Little House on the Prairie" would call it "first light") she would snatch the sheets from under you, not only inconveniencing you but shaming you as well. She had been up for hours, had perked the coffee and started the grits. You were positively slovenly if you slept past six. She washed with Tag soap and used a bluing water for the second rinse. I think it was my aunt Agnes who purchased a wringer washer for her. No one knows what that is anymore. The clothes washed electronically—that is, the tub would spin and churgle all by itself, but it wouldn't wring the clothes dry; you had to hand-feed them through the wringer. I guess some of the things we have today, that we, in fact, take for granted, were unheard of in Emma Lou's day. On the other hand, women did real work. All this talk about feeling useless was such nonsense. If clichés have any truck with reality, certainly "A woman's work is never done" is true. It was always a pleasure to watch her wipe her hands on her apron at day's end, take a cigarette from Grandpapa's package, and sit down. The footstool on which she rested her feet is in my bedroom right now. I don't have a fireplace, but the glow from 400 Mulvaney is in my heart.

Grandmothers are special. They talk funny; they think differently; and they are always telling us how much easier we have it. I'm not so sure. But when I began to think about the grandmother experience again, I wrote a lot of friends and asked if they would share their experiences. Grandmothers, it seems, are a lot like spinach or asparagus or brussels sprouts: something good for us that we appreciate much more in reflection' than in actuality. We were all young when we met these women; we were teenagers by the time we learned to resent their easy, almost casual way of telling us what to do and how to do it. On top of that we had to hear how they and our parents had done everything better. Personally speaking, I'm glad I'm not a teenager anymore. All those emotions running around; all that trying to be grown yet never knowing what "grown" is. It helps tremendously, I think, to just learn that "grown" is something between who we, teenagers, are and who our grandmothers are. Grandmothers make those transitions for us. And they are always on our side. There were, however, times when my grandmother wanted me to pour tea at the church program and I pouted, asking her, "Why do I have to waste my Sunday afternoon?" And there were times when I had to visit the sick, run errands for her friends (and you were *not* allowed to take any money for it), redo a chore that was adequately if not expertly done, and I wondered what is it with grandmothers. Mother would have accepted "No" or "Not yet" for an answer. Grandmother wanted it *now*. And cheerfully. Grandmother helped me become civilized. She helped me see that little things are all that matter. She taught me patience. She showed me how to create beauty in everything I do.

Not all grandmothers are the same; maybe yours were the ones to let you off easy, and your parents set the rules. But they are always important, and that is why I asked friends to write in this book. If a book is going to be about someone who is as important to us as a grandmother, then the entire book should be friendly. That doesn't mean nice and easy, though. Grandmothers are older than we are, they have to be, and we grow up with them, even if that means having to take over being an adult too soon. They teach us even when they leave us behind.

I don't know, personally, all the writers in this book, but I do know Maxine Hong Kingston and I know that she is magical, so it did not surprise me that her grandmother is really a grandfather who longed for a daughter and since he produced only sons had to turn himself into his own creation. I share a birthday with Gwendolyn Brooks, which *we* share with Prince, and I would never dream of doing this book without asking her for a contribution. Gwen was, in fact, my first acceptance and I said to myself: If a writer as busy and important as Gwen Brooks can answer right away, I must be on the right track. Gloria Naylor is another friend. My mother made beans for her recently. Grandmother was a great cook with fancy meats and pastries, but my mother makes the world's greatest beans. She is our secret weapon and we don't often share her. Gloria was talking about how much she loved beans and Mommy said, "I'll make you some in the morning. *If you will get me a piece of salt pork.*" My mother is straight out of the Labors of Hercules or Jason or some Greek sort of thing. She is the good fairy who makes you do the one thing that is damned difficult to do, so I helped Gloria out by magically producing salt pork from my freezer, where I had squirreled it away when Mommy said she was coming to visit. Mother made the world's greatest black beans, and while it would be unfair to say Gloria wrote about her Mississippi grandmothers because of it . . . well, you've just gotta believe in magic.

This is not a balanced book. We are mostly Southern,

pan Asian, and black. What I hope this book will show others is that like Alex Haley, who created the wonderful *Roots* from stories he heard his grandmother tell, we all have grandmother stories. Speaking of my mother, by the way, this collection ends with her first published essay, "Mama Dear," which is about her grandmother, Cornelia Watson. I was given her first name as my middle name.

For the last five years I have been privileged to work with a retirement center, Warm Hearth. I thought we should have some stories *from* grandmothers in the book, too. We are about fourteen seniors who range in age from the middle seventies to the late nineties. The Warm Hearth Writers Workshop has published one book, *Appalachian Elders: A Warm Hearth Sampler,* and one member, Ellison Smythe, has published his own book, *Retrospect.* Ellison, in fact, was so upset when I invited the ladies of the workshop to contribute to this book that he wrote about his grandmother in protest. Being an old protester myself, I could not resist including him. The Warm Hearth grandmothers go back beyond the Civil War. One member had a Yankee and a Confederate grandmother; others had grandmothers who were immigrants who could not speak the language of their husbands. All were young women with dreams of a new country, a new life in their hearts. They had to dream of us.

"A Loss in Detroit" is a special story to me because grandmothers don't just make wonderful cookies and give us dimes for learning state capitals. Though most teenagers have not been divorced, sometimes our parents have, and even we have broken up with girlfriends and boyfriends. We lose or drop friends of the same or different sex all through our lives. Sometimes a girlfriend is, say, shoplifting and we don't want to do that. Even though our relationship

is not romantic, when we decide to break off that friendship, it's a kind of divorce, and there is pain and questioning.
If our friend wants to try drugs and we know better than
that, we experience a kind of divorce when we know we
will not "hang" with that person again. "Loss in Detroit" is
about a husband leaving and the grandmother pretending
she cannot remember who the granddaughter married in
the first place. Grandmothers put quilts over us and let us
curl upon the couch and rock ourselves to sleep. While no
one is advocating divorce, of the alternatives of parting,
divorce makes more sense than, say, murder. I know everyone talks about fortitude and sticking it out, and if there is
one group who mean "forever," grandmothers are certainly
that group. Yet we learn to live with mistakes by admitting
them; we learn that pencils have erasers for a reason. It's so
sane, don't you know? Not all of us like our grandmothers,
and I should imagine not all of our grandmothers like us . . .
but we are tied together in a generational struggle from
which no loser and therefore no winner can emerge.

When I actually contemplate my grandmother, Emma
Lou, the image that stays in my mind is the one that always
makes me cry. She was nineteen years old when she married
John Brown Watson. She was in her late fifties when he
died. She had spent most of her life rearing three daughters,
seeing all three receive degrees from Knoxville College; she
had been faithful to her church, Mt. Zion Baptist Church;
she was an avid club woman, from a supporter of Delta
Sigma Theta to her book club, the bridge club, the Court of
Calanthe, the Colored Women's Federated Clubs, the
flower club, and any and all political groups to help uplift
the Negro; she loved to laugh. Yet after we buried Grandpapa, she stood alone at the top of the first set of stairs to
wave good-bye to Mommy, Chris, my nephew, and me, as

we were the last to leave, and it struck me how alone, not only she, but all of us are. If she contemplated death, and I have every reason to think she surely must have (she lost her mother the same year she married John Brown, and Mama Dear became the mother she did not have), she must have realized that one day she would be there on that hill alone. But it wasn't fair. All of her life she had been in the service of her God, her husband, her children, that which was right. Yet none of us could replace what she was losing. She waved that brave wave that my mother has, which is why when I am leaving my mother I go late at night or early in the morning so that I do not have to see the question on her face: Will you return safely to me? We sang, at her funeral, "It Is Well With My Soul"; the preacher said, "Well done, my good and faithful servant." But that does nothing to fill the void in me. So this isn't a balanced book nor a sociological book nor a look at grandmothers through the ages. It's just a book that makes me miss the only person I know for sure whose love I did not have to earn.

GRAND MOTHERS

PART ONE

". . . What are you talkin' 'bout did I love you?
Girl, I stayed alive for you."

—TONI MORRISON

My Grandmother Is Waiting for Me to Come Home

By Gwendolyn Brooks

My grandmother is waiting for me to come home.
We live with walnuts and apples
in a one-room kitchenette above The
Some Day Liquor Gardens.

My grandmother sits in a red rocking chair
waiting for me
to open the door with my key.

She is black and glossy like coal.

We eat walnuts and apples,
drink root beer in cups that are broken
above The
Some Day Liquor Gardens.

I love my grandmother.
She is wonderful to behold
with the glossy of her coal-colored skin.
She is warm wide and long.
She laughs and she lingers.

Listening With Her Heart

By *Virginia C. Fowler*

What the dead had no speech for, when living,
They can tell you, being dead: the communication
Of the dead is tongued with fire beyond the
language of the living.
—T. S. Eliot

My grandmother's importance in my life has always been obvious to those who know me well, if only from her predominance in the collage of snapshots that decorates my study wall. Amongst her grandchildren, I hold an honored—though, ironically, not envied—status resulting from my having lived with her during my four years of college. Remembered by everyone as the dominating matriarch of the family, my grandmother still controls her children, themselves now grandparents. But because I lived with her and was her grandchild, not her child, she was never able to silence me in the way she silenced my mother; indeed, we argued frequently and vigorously during the years we lived together, and I often find myself, to my dismay, speaking with her sharp tongue as well as exercising her quick wit.

Because we shared a close relationship, I imagined that writing about her would be, if not easy, at least possible. But when one aborted effort after another began to fill my hard disk, I realized that I had a problem. At first, I thought it was a writing problem. Then I thought it was perhaps a memory problem. It seemed that all my memories of her were vague, blurred, out of focus. Yet when I tried to sharpen and clarify them, she refused three-dimensionality, would not assume a form that fit with the many complex emotions she provoked in me. Instead, like characters in a B-grade movie, either she or I was consistently villainous. In one memory, she played the part of a tyrannical matriarch, while in the next I would appear as selfish, spoiled, petulant. In none of the scenes I recalled did there appear more than a hint of the gifts she gave me, of the real emotions she generated in me, or of the significant influence she has had in my life. So I set aside my hopelessly distorted, specific memories and focused instead on two images that together represent my grandmother.

My grandmother was deaf through much of her adult life and blind during her last twenty years. As both an avid conversationalist and a voracious reader, she could hardly have been sent more difficult trials. Yet I have never known anyone less daunted by what can be crippling disabilities. And the more I have pondered my two mental photographs of her, the more I have come to realize how completely they capture the *resistance* to adversity that is one of her greatest legacies to me.

In the first photograph, she sits on the old stepchair in the kitchen, typing away on her antique Underwood—writing one of the letters that gained her the reputation of being a wonderful correspondent. She has just sat back down after answering the phone, or perhaps pouring a cup of coffee, and is unable to see where she left off. I stand behind her, looking over her shoulder to see the last words she typed. Sometimes in my photograph I am looking at a page on which the imprint of the typewriter keys is terribly faint; the characters are uninked. Her ribbon, used way beyond its reasonable life span, has literally given up the ghost. I am breaking the news to her that, after I change the ribbon for her, she will have to begin her letter all over again.

In the second photograph, she again sits on the step-chair, but this time in the hallway off the kitchen, talking on the telephone. She wears an old-fashioned hearing aid clipped to her armored corset, the cord wound inge-niously and unobtrusively around the back of her neck, under her hair, into her ear. She holds the telephone receiver upside down, the hearing part pressed to the general vicinity of her heart, the speaking part held to her mouth as a singer might hold a microphone. This image informs my earliest memories of her; I grew up convinced that she listened with something deep inside of her, her heart or her soul, rather than her ears.

As I reflect on the first photograph, I find an instructive lesson for my efforts to write about my grandmother. Hav-ing received many imprinted but uninked letters from her, both before and after I lived with her, I know that what mattered was not the interesting tidbits of gossip or philo-sophical meanderings that I tried in vain to decipher. What mattered, of course, was that she was thinking about me, reaching out to speak to me, to communicate, to remind me that she was there for me. (Like for most women of her generation, long-distance telephone calls were reserved for very special occasions and were strictly limited to the sacred three minutes.) I have often thought that had her children been able to understand the real message of love underlying the sharp and dictatorial words she often spoke to them, they would have been freed from behavior she didn't really want from them anyway. Happily, I was in fact able to do so. She might ask me unceasingly when I was going to find a husband, but her sitting up late to listen to my college papers told me quite clearly that she believed in me and my ability to do something beyond getting married and having children.

The second photograph likewise reminds me that communication involves something beyond what the eye can see or the ear can hear. I was never amazed by one of the family legends regarding my grandmother's deafness. She was quite unable to hear anything after she took her hearing aid off at night. Yet in the middle of the night on which my grandfather lay dying in the hospital, she got up to go to the bathroom and, passing the telephone, felt certain that it was ringing. She placed her hands on it, felt the vibration, answered it, and ran for her hearing aid. It was indeed the hospital with the news she had been dreading.

To me, this episode was not all that remarkable, given who my grandmother was. I will always believe that it really was her heart that heard our calls and our cries, not that little Zenith box that whistled and screeched when the batteries were low or the volume was too high. As I always suspected, and since her death have come to know with certainty, she communicated on another frequency altogether.

A Conspiracy of Grace

❧

By Ethel Morgan Smith

Big Mama knew everything and everybody, and no one
held it against her. She was a sin eater and a joy giver. Lying,
however, was not a sin she was willing to eat. "One lie just
make ways to break all of the other rules of the Lord," she
always said. Because of Big Mama's strict adherence to the
truth, I grew up with no belief in childhood figures like
Santa Claus or the Easter Bunny.

After being married to Grandpa Alex for fifty-three
years, she left him to spend the rest of her days in peace.
Then Grandpa Alex went on a drinking spree and was
struck by a car. She moved back home and took care of him
until he died.

A day after he was buried, the white man they had
sharecropped for came to the house and asked Big Mama
who was going to farm the land. She looked him in the eye
without blinking and said, "My husband ain't cold in his
grave, and you come here and show no respect for him or
the Lord. We farmed that sorry land for more than forty
years, and I 'spect it'll keep bein' worked."

The white man left without saying a word. Later he spread the word around town: "Never cross that woman."

Big Mama moved in with us when I was four. It gave Mother the means and courage to put Mr. Tex out of our house and out of our lives. He was my sisters' father, my mother's third husband, and everybody's disappointment.

Mother worked two jobs and Big Mama was in charge of domestic relations at our house. I mostly remember the winters, when steamed windowpanes were juicy like fresh blackberries. The round table graced the middle of the worn plank floor. Buttery smells, sweet smells, and sometimes smoky smells draped the room, and held on to it like there would be no tomorrow. When the wind blew the wrong way, the smoke burned our eyes. If the smoke lingered long, we went to our room and closed the door and put a towel at the bottom of it. Sometimes before a rain, the smell of red clay quietly slipped through the house. It eased all of our immediate pains. Then the rain came. The first sign would be the pitty-pat sound on the tin roof. Then we saw it on the windowpanes; it was like a member of the family. We never worked when thunder or lightning crackled through the house, because Big Mama said, "When the Good Lord is carryin' on His work, we oughta show some respect."

Everyone in the community called her "Miss Mag." She was a giant of a woman, with paper-sack brown skin that was smooth as a summer peach. For Big Mama, visiting the sick was just as natural as wearing her apron every day. She often gave more respect to people when they were sick or dead than when they were alive and well. When Miss Cora Lee Jackson's left leg was amputated because she was bitten by a rattlesnake, Big Mama sat with her for three days. She bathed her and fanned the flies away. None of Miss Cora

Lee's family would sit with her, because they said the smell made them sick. Even Doctor Norton wouldn't visit her without a mask.

Taking care of the sick was a major part of living in our community. Doctor Norton came every other Thursday. In between times babies were born, accidents happened, children had measles, mumps, chicken pox, and colds, and old people died. If a place was too far to walk to, Big Mama hitched her mule and wagon. We never knew when she would return, but we never worried about her safety; a double-barreled shotgun and two boxes of shells were always at her side.

We always knew when Big Mama was planning a sick journey. She would put a kettle of water on the stove to boil for the scalding of the feathers on a chicken. She could wring a chicken's neck without flinching. Afterward she would throw the chicken in the backyard; my sisters and I clapped to the rhythm of the dying chicken. When the chicken finally died, we put it in a tin tub and poured the boiling water on it. Another kettle of water was put on the stove; the children plucked the chicken the first time and Big Mama completed the task. She worked harder than anyone I knew, and had the appetite to prove it. She could eat one-half of a chicken at one sitting.

Her hazelnut brown eyes were mostly kind, but if you looked deep enough, you could see the pain that was there. She bore twelve children, and only Mother lived. She never spoke of her pain. We knew about the dead babies from the Bible on the living room table. We never discussed anything with Big Mama, because her philosophy was that children should be seen and not heard.

After one of her sick trips, she was particularly demanding about our chores. I always wanted to know what happened to the sick person. She would look at me and say, "That's grown folks' business, gal." Later, at supper, she would say, "We saved him/her." "We" meant that the Lord was the main caretaker and she was only a helper.

Big Mama wasn't big on going to church. She only went to funerals. "The Good Lord can hear me anywhere," she said. "Just a bunch of showy hypocrites, sittin' in the amen corner. It don't mean nothin' what other folks thank of you, it's what *you* thank of you that counts."

When my sisters and I did our schoolwork, we sat around a big oak kitchen table that was covered with a scruffy oilcloth. Big Mama sat in the corner by the stove in a rocking chair that had been painted so many times, no one remembered the original color. What I do remember is that it swayed a bit to the left.

Her hair was like gray corn silk. Often it was parted in the middle. She only washed it in rainwater because, she said, "it was a gift directly from the Lord." Her spit can was always nearby, because she was never without a dip of Honey Bee snuff. While we studied, the only sound in the room was that of her cutting okra or shelling peas. Sometimes she hummed "Down by the River Side" or "Amazing Grace." Her voice was as strong as a Georgia pine. I was the arithmetic whiz, my sister Lela was the queen of English, and Hannah was an ace at science. Big Mama was always the boss. At the end of our two-hour study period, I always went first because I was the oldest. We stood directly in front of her with our right hand locked in the left. Our shoulders were straight and we were expected to stand tall. Big Mama asked questions that seemed endless. They always began with "What was you 'pose to do? Did you know how to do it?" If there was no schoolwork, we had to read a book. The questions then were "Who wrote the book?" and "Did it teach you anything about being a better person?" Some days she wanted to know who in the book we liked best and how come. Sometimes she wanted to know the same kinds of things about our teachers. These questions were only asked when all of the assignments were completed. We had to raise our hands to get permission to speak. Hannah had big red curly braids, and it had taken three years for her front teeth to grow in. She thought she was smarter than anyone. Once, and only once, she tried to vex Big Mama. Later, Hannah told us it was a lot easier to just do your schoolwork. The sugarberry switches in the corner were good reminders of that.

My sister Lela was tall, lanky, and a little shy. Big Mama yelled at her, "Stand up straight. We ain't into reading your mind, you know" or "Can you speak louder?" When Big Mama wasn't around, Lela giggled a lot.

When Miss Lucy Mae, our neighbor, had to work late, her son Roy waited at our house. Roy was always mad when he had to sit around the table and study, but the sugarberry branches in the corner kept him from fretting too much either.

Roy would rather have stayed at Miss Lucille's because they had a new floor-model television, but Miss Lucille didn't want anything to do with Roy, because she thought his daddy was Mr. Limberman, the white man who ran the store on Junction Road.

Big Mama said she was glad that Mr. Jake, Miss Lucy Mae's husband, wasn't Roy's daddy because Roy's brother Junior was dumber than dirt, and was the only child she knew who repeated the first grade three times. "I don't know what high horse Lucille is ridin'. Dat TV gone plumb to her head. If Lucy Mae is going wit Old Man Limberman, I hope she's gettin' a good cut of meat for her trouble."

We children weren't allowed to repeat such gossip. I remember Mother once said, "It's hard to tell from looking at Roy. He was red-brown in color, but that didn't tell you much of nothing."

"Dat's just it," Big Mama said. "None of them look like much. But I know one thing, Lucy Mae ain't never told me a lie. Lucille cheated me out of thirteen cents in 1941, and that's all I need to know."

Often during supper, Big Mama and Mother argued about who worked harder. No one ever won; it was always to be continued. Sometimes the insurance man interrupted our supper. Once when he did, Mother looked at Big Mama and said, "I know how to get rid of him." Big Mama nodded with approval.

Mother went into the front room to greet him. We continued to eat, but the kitchen was only a few feet away, so we could easily hear them.

"Maudie, I want to tell you about a new program we have," the insurance man said.

"Have you ever been to New York?" Mother asked.

"No, can't say that I have. This new program is only good for this month."

"I took the Greyhound bus to New York City to visit Cousin Beuford when he was in the hospital," Mother said.

"That's nice, Maudie," the insurance man said before she could hardly finish.

"It's funny. That was ten years ago, but everyone up there called me Mrs. Baker."

"That's nice, Maudie, but I want to explain this new program to you."

By the time Mother got to the part about whites and coloreds living side by side in New York City, the insurance man would be ready to leave.

Mother came back to the supper table and looked in the direction of Big Mama, and Big Mama nodded with approval again. My sisters and I always giggled, and Big Mama reminded us that having enough burial insurance was not a laughing matter. She said that Mr. Pig Walker hadn't left enough burial insurance, and his family had to take up an offering at his funeral; Mr. Pig Walker was still turning over in his grave because of the disgrace. We always wanted to giggle when Big Mama got to that part.

Finally Big Mama and Mother would pick up their discussion about who worked harder. After supper my sisters and I washed, dried, and put away the dishes, and then we went to bed. I've never felt safer than I did when my sisters and I washed dishes after supper, particularly when the insurance man disrupted us without saying "Excuse me," or asking permission to come another time. Big Mama and Mother seemed so powerful to me. They allowed no one to disrupt our lives, not even white folks.

When we were growing up, it was Big Mama who did most of the mothering. Mother distanced herself from us. I accepted it simply because we always had Big Mama. And, of course, it never entered my mind to question our family. It wasn't until I was a grown-up that I dared to question Mother's distance. But there was only silence.

Big Mama was very protective of Mother. Mother was physically and spiritually distant from my sisters and me. She had the ability to ruin any holiday for us. I accepted her grief and tried to give her room to grieve because I knew her pain was about her firstborn, Mary Lisa, who died at age seven from spinal meningitis, before I was born. Mother never stopped grieving and Big Mama never stopped protecting her. It was not until my own son was born that I had any kind of understanding of their conspiracy.

When I arrived home from the hospital after the birth of my son, Big Mama was most thankful for her first great-grandson. She said, "Now you may have more heart for your mama. You can dream what it may be like to bury your firstborn." She was talking about all of her pain, too, wrapped up in those eleven babies she had buried. From that moment on I forgave Mother for her distance, and I was thankful for Big Mama.

It never occurred to me that Big Mama would die, but she did. When it happened, folks far and near heard the news, and within hours they found their way to Miss Mag's—Babe Baxter's youngest daughter—with their Sunday-best lemon pound cakes and banana puddings in rough, worn pie pans. But none brought Ice Box Pie. Only Big Mama knew the recipe. Over the years it had graced the table of many of the fine eateries in our community. But that day it was missed, just like the old wrinkled hands that could make Ice Box Pie in her sleep. We wept, we hugged, we laughed, we remembered, but mostly we were thankful. I found comfort in the stories that lingered through the house about Miss Mag. The peaceful breeze was balmy.

I remembered most of the women from my childhood. They were all heavier and grayer than they used to be, and had fewer teeth, but their eyes were as sincere as ever. I recall so clearly the solid expressions on their faces, the sadness in their eyes, and the genuine love and affection they expressed for Big Mama. They were about to lay to rest an institution.

Some gathered in the kitchen. A chunky, chocolate-brown woman introduced herself to me as Miss Mattie Pearl. She told of an unusually cold Christmas when she had no food or Santa Claus for her five children, and hadn't seen her husband in a long time, and any other family she had was in the same bind. With tears in her stormy, soot-black eyes, the woman turned to me. "Honey, your grandma was the sweetest people I know of. 'Cause of her, that Christmas turned magic. She showed up on our door-step on that Christmas Eve with your mama's boys totin' two big cardboard boxes. Paid no mind to the cold. Even said Christmases ought to be cold. She pulled out pecan cakes, apples and oranges, a roasted hen, and a small wrapped present for each one of us."

The stories continued; I drifted from corner to corner of the overflowing house. Snowball, a smooth-skinned, grayish-black woman I'd known all of my life, was there. "Child, for the first time in the South, as low as us on the map, it snowed like we was way up North. We had six inches," she told me with a slight stutter. "The doctor couldn't make it to our house when Mama's water broke and the pains started whippin' her. She sent my older sisters five houses down the road to get Miss Mag." Snowball stopped in the middle of her story and took sips from her Mason jar full of iced tea before continuing. Her chunky chocolate fingers were sweating; she caught her breath and wiped her tears. "Y'all know the rest of the story, and I ain't never been as proud to have the name Snowball as I is this day."

"Miss Mag was the only one I would count on, too," said a short plump woman with curly hair and a small baby on her wide right hip. The baby played with her mama's hair; they had the same curls. "Miss Maggie come in my room and put those warm and wrinkled hands on my shoulders. She told me she knowed it was hard for me, but we had to do what we had to do, and the Good Lord was gonna to be with us. Me and Miss Maggie buried my firstborn."

As some friends left, others arrived, bearing their favorite potato salad or more crispy fried chicken. In the living room, a small bushy-haired woman took slow bites of her lemon cheesecake and told her story, with her head thrown back and her eyes set toward the heavens. "I walked way over five miles that hot and hazy summer day. It was hot August dog days. I axed Miss Mag if she thought I was with my first child. She looked me straight in the eye and said, 'You probably is.' I thought I was gonna die and go to hell. 'Go talk to the father and work things out,' Miss Mag told me. 'Chullins is the most precious of the gifts the Lord can give us on earth. Count your blessins and be a good mother to your child.' "

"You too, honey?" said a woman with a wrinkled taupe-colored pleated dress and glasses practically hanging off her nose. "That lady was my anchor. I just knowed my world was over, knowing Papa would put me out of the house and everything, and warn't sure Jake would marry me. I just wanted to disappear. Miss Mag would hear none of that nonsense. 'The world is a beautiful place,' she said. 'Just 'cause this is a particular bad time ain't no reason to give it up. Remember the good times.' Then she sort of half-laughed, and said, 'Like the time the baby was made.' "

Every person there under the age of sixty could probably remember at least one good spanking by those creased, strong hands. Our house had been the neighborhood day-care center. There was no money involved. Big Mama offered love and discipline, and the children gave love and respect.

Around midnight, when the stories ended, the loving friends left, and we all made the first step toward getting on with our lives. The immediate family gathered in her bedroom. Here's My Heart cologne lingered softly in the air; a thick breath of witch hazel lotion offset the sweetness of the cologne. I felt closer to Big Mama, at least for a long second.

We eased through her belongings, finding lace hankies, peppermint candy, our elementary-school photos, snuff in a rusted-top can. There were fircrackers, good and every-day underwear, neat stacks of greeting cards, and obituaries of friends and relatives. She had been very proud of the fact that her burial insurance had been paid off for many years.

My sisters and I selected small items, very ceremoniously. We realized the value of our legacy. In that small paneled room with the light-blue sheer curtains and the matching ruffled spread on the white iron bed, we realized that Big Mama would always be a part of us. And I realized that some of the most valuable lessons I'd learned came from an old woman who couldn't read or write and didn't even know her real birthday.

Her funeral was a few days later. The small, square-shaped church with its green walls and thin mismatched carpet seemed exactly the same as it had been when I was a child. The ceiling fans were on full speed, and ushers wear-ing white gloves passed out all of the cardboard fans. The heat and steam would not let go of their grip on the room. Grown men cried like babies. The front of the church was loaded with colorful flowers, both artificial and real. Elderly sisters, many with crutches, rose from each corner of the church to speak kind words. When I thought of the funeral afterward, it was very fragmented and hazy. Mourners were as far back as I was able to see. The minister bcame so emotional while conducting the service that Deacon Evans had to assist him to his seat. Reverend Struggs pulled out his starched white handkerchief and shook sweat beads that looked like large teardrops from his face. His cloudy eyes turned bloodshot. Instead of feeling sad, I felt proud. Big Mama would have loved that moment of her funeral the most. She loved funerals and had been preparing for hers since I could remember. It all seemed so natural.

The Roofwalker

By Susan Power

It was family legend that Grandma Mabel Rattles Chasing came down from Standing Rock Reservation in North Dakota to help deliver me. She took the Greyhound bus all the way to Chicago, stepping out of the exhaust fumes like a ghost emerging from fog, her deep paper shopping bags banging against the sides of her legs. For most of the trip she had been finishing a child-sized star quilt, touching the fabric as gently as she would her new grandchild, smoothing it in her lap. This was the quilt they would wrap me in after my first bath, the same quilt Mom pulled out in later years every time I was sick.

Grandma Mabel came to help with the delivery because my mother was terrified of going to the huge maternity ward at Chicago's Cook County Hospital. She was convinced that the white doctors would sterilize her after she gave birth, a practice once routine at many reservation hospitals. So I was born in our third-floor apartment, which was little more than a chain of narrow rooms, resembling the cars of a train.

Family legend continued that I began life with a fall. My birth went smoothly until Grandma Mabel wiped my face and head with her hands. What she saw made her scream, and I slipped out of her fingers like buttered dough. My father caught me. He went down on one knee and his slim hands with long fingers stretched beneath me like a net.

"What is it?! What's wrong?!" I can imagine Mom's voice getting frantic as she tried to sit up, afraid I was born with too many fingers, or too few toes.

"Nothing, just her hair. It's different," Dad told her.

"The color of the devil," Grandma whispered, and they made her sit down because she was trembling.

As far back as anyone in my family could remember, both sides were Indian: full-blood Sioux on my mother's side and full-blood Sioux on Dad's. Yet I was born with red hair the color of autumn maple leaves. Grandma Mabel looked at me sideways and began to recite stories of the Viking invaders.

"Hundreds of years ago, long before Columbus and his three boats got lost and stumbled upon our land, those Vikings came down from the North country, where it's always cold. They had red hair and blue eyes, and heavy hatchets made of bronze. They married into our tribes. They must have. Just look." Grandma Mabel brushed my head with the tips of her fingers.

Although I was the mysterious family skeleton pushed out of the closet with my mother's fluid still damp on my skin, Grandma Mabel didn't hold it against me for long. Soon she was cradling me in her broad lap, her round thighs ample as pillows. She traced my features with a thick finger, smoothing my forehead when it wrinkled in frustrated hunger. I know this because I have seen the photographs. I spent years playing with them, spreading them out on the coffee table. Grandma Mabel's skin was brown and wrinkled as a walnut, but her hair was mostly black, tied in one long braid. She wore shapeless cotton dresses and bowling sneakers, and I noticed that her legs looked strong but lumpy, a little like caked oatmeal. I knew her eyes were black, because Mom told me, but in the photographs it was impossible to tell. Grandma Mabel's eyes were so bright they were beams of light shooting from her face, making me blink if I stared at them for too long.

Grandma Mabel was a presence in my life even though she returned to the reservation shortly after I was born. I came to know her through the photographs and the occasional phone calls she made from her tiny government-funded house. The stories she told me over the phone were better than the ones Mom told me at night before I fell asleep. Grandma asked me strange questions sometimes.

"Do you have spiders in Chicago?" she asked me once.

"Sure we do."

"I hope you don't kill them. You have to be careful because one of them might be Iktóme."

"Who's that?" I asked her, smiling to myself because I knew the answer would involve a story.

"He is a spirit and sometimes he takes the form of a spider. He is clever-foolish, like your little brothers."

I knew what she meant. By this time I had two younger brothers, Billy and Grover, both of them as dark as our parents and Grandma Mabel, unburdened by my mysterious red hair, and both of them were energetically mischievous.

"Iktóme is greedy," Grandma Mabel continued. "That's the bad side of him. If he has a plump duck or a haunch of venison set for dinner and he sees a chance to get something more, he will go after it. But you know what happens when he does that? Coyote sneaks behind him and steals the fat duck or the juicy venison and runs off with it. Then Iktóme goes hungry."

"Grandma, I wish you were here," I told her one time. I wanted the stories to last longer. I wanted her shining eyes to light my room at bedtime like two candles burning in the dark.

"I know it," she said. "It's hard."

"Why do we live in Chicago?" I finally asked my mother after one particularly entertaining visit with Grandma Mabel, when she told me she could hear her husband's ghost singing to her from the bottom of their old well.

"Your father's job is here," Mom told me.

"Can't he work somewhere else?"

"It's not that easy." Mom sighed. "He's a political person, and political people don't always have a lot of choices."

My mother chose her words cautiously, I could tell. She spoke slowly and the words seemed heavy as she spoke them, like dense marbles rolling off her tongue. There were other times when she flung words at my father and wasn't careful at all. She'd point to him and tell us: "Your father is a gung-ho Indian. It's his job and his life!"

We were living in the uptown area of Chicago, just blocks away from the Indian Center on Wilson Avenue, which is where Dad went to work each day. I knew that he wrote proposals for the Indian community, but when I was little I didn't understand what that meant. I imagined my father writing marriage proposals for shy Indian men who couldn't find the words for themselves, who would have spent their lives alone were it not for my father's intervention. Likewise, I didn't know what a gung-ho Indian was, but in retrospect, I suppose my father fits that description. He always wore jeans, cowboy boots, a Western shirt with silver clips on the collar, and a heavy turquoise bolo tie. He never carried a briefcase but instead used an old backpack completely covered by pins and bumper stickers with slogans like: CUSTER DIED FOR YOUR SINS, I'M SIOUX AND PROUD, INDIAN POWER, and POWWOW COUNTRY.

Dad burned tobacco on Columbus Day to mourn the arrival of the man who pressed Indians into slavery, fasted on Thanksgiving Day to show his solidarity with all those eastern tribes the Pilgrims killed off with their European strain of germs, and set off fireworks on June 26 to celebrate the anniversary of the Little Big Horn battle, when our ancestors crushed Custer like a wood tick.

I asked Grandma Mabel what it all meant.

"What is a gung-ho Indian?"

"Well . . ." She paused then and I could hear her sipping liquid, probably wild peppermint tea, which she said kept her blood healthy. "That's a good question. It used to be that your people knew who they were and what was expected of them. From the time they were born, each day was a lesson. They were close to the father over all of us— Wakán Tánka, the one who hears our prayers. But we have gone through many things and now it's difficult to find the right road. Some of our people try too hard; they think they've found the old-time trail leading them to the heart of our traditions, but if they looked down, I think they would see only their footprints. It is their own lonely trail, and they are truly lost."

Was my father lost? I wanted to call him back and take him by the hand. I would walk with him, eyes cast upon the ground, looking for signs that other Sioux people had passed this way before us. I didn't want him to wander all alone, carrying nothing but his worn backpack and an angry heart.

．　．　．

When I was nine years old Dad left us. My brothers and I were like those three blind mice: we didn't see it coming. I think my mother did. I am certain now that Mom could read this future in my father's face because when the time came, she simply lived through it. She had probably noticed the way women watched my handsome father, who was tall and straight, with brown skin smooth as glass and wavy long hair streaming down his back.

Of course, Dad didn't tell us there was another woman but blamed politics for our separation. He said he was going back to his own reservation in South Dakota—Pine Ridge—where so much trouble was brewing.

"I can make a difference," he said.

My mother wasn't fooled for a second. "Then take us with you," she told him.

"It's not that easy," my father answered. "These days Pine Ridge is dangerous, Indians fighting Indians and the FBI just complicating everything. I can't take you back there."

Dad bought a used Volkswagen van and painted bronze fists on each of its sides. At first I admired it, imagined it reflected his conscience and principles; it was a rugged little vehicle, hell-bent for danger and activism. But then my mother pointed out the truth with her chin as we watched it from our apartment window. My father had a young girl with hair as long as his own already living in that van.

I decided to investigate, and when Mom was busy preparing lunch for me and my brothers, I ran down the front stairs. The girl was standing outside the van, leaning against it with her arms crossed. She was watching our apartment window three stories above her with muddy green eyes the color of the Chicago River. She's only a part-blood Indian, like me, I thought. She had on hip-hugger jeans with wide bell-bottoms that dragged on the ground, covering her feet.

On top she wore a skimpy halter hanging loosely from her narrow, caved-in chest. I knew she was observing me, too, although she never glanced away from the window. I was in the doorway of our building, right in front of her, staring rudely, which I had been taught never to do.

Finally she asked, "Which one are you?"

"Jessie," I told her. I pulled myself a little straighter and wiped the limp red bangs from my forehead.

"Oh," she said. She shrugged her right shoulder and lifted suddenly on tiptoes to get a better view of our apartment. Just as I was about to leave, pushing back against the outside glass door, she looked at me again. Her green eyes fell on mine like heavy hammers. I couldn't blink, my eyes were dry, her hard look was squeezing the breath from my lungs. My fingernails cut into my palms.

"I love him," she said. We stood there silently for a while.

Finally I whispered, "I love him, too." My voice was gentle but it wasn't out of kindness or sympathy. Anger sizzled in the pit of my stomach; I felt the sparks fly inside of me, scorching my heart and lungs. She turned her back on me, retreating into the safety of the van.

I walked to the back of the building and sat on the porch steps. I wished I could become a bird of vengeance. I pointed my toes inside my sneakers, feeling their terrible grip, and imagined the fierce sweep they would make at that part-blood girl's hair. My talons would tangle in her hair like barbed wire and I would carry her off, banging her useless, scrawny body against the building as I flew toward the lake. Halfway to Canada maybe I would let her go, hovering in the air so I could watch her fall into the deep cold center of Lake Michigan. Her heavy, angry eyes would weight her down like stones. She would never float or be recovered.

As the bird of vengeance, I would shriek and cackle, loud enough so that my mother would hear it and know she was avenged, powerful enough so that my father would hear me and know that I had won.

The day finally came for my father to leave. My mother sat on one of the kitchen chairs. For the first time I noticed that the chair she always used was the one repaired with black electric tape, just as she always set herself the chipped plate and bent fork. Dad was standing with one pointy-toed boot resting on a chair, his body hitched over the bent knee. My parents faced slightly apart and I remember worrying that they wouldn't be able to hear each other, that their words would slide in different directions.

"Let's not put the kids through a big scene," Dad told her.

Mom's dry eyes hurt me more than if they had been pouring tears like the Hoover Dam burst open. She didn't flinch or rustle but was suddenly still and massive, the center of gravity become flesh in our kitchen.

"It doesn't matter what I say or what I do," she finally said, and I was convinced that her voice slipped out of her navel and not from her thin, pressed lips.

Was that all she was going to say? I was trembling, as nervous as she was motionless; my blood was sliding too quickly through my veins. I wanted to scream: *Stop him! Don't let him go!* But I had been raised too well for that. Instead I bit my tongue until I tasted blood.

Dad moved then, walked toward my mother. He scooped her hand into his but almost lost it, it was so heavy.

"You're a good woman," he said, "and I promise I'll call you. Take care of yourself." He kissed her on the cheek and replaced her hand. He was on his way out. He looked so relieved when he said his last words: "I just have to do some things that are bigger than my life."

"Don't kid yourself," Mom answered.

I know Dad must have hugged and kissed the three of us before he made it out the front door. After all, we stood there in the hallway between the kitchen and living room, his last hurdle to freedom. But I don't remember it. I must have blanked it out. Or maybe I was frightened because his last touch was too much like a ghost walking right through me.

I remember looking out of the front window, my mother suddenly beside me. She took my hand and I realized she was facing the wrong way, her back was to the street.

"Has he gone?" she asked me. I looked out and saw the painted upraised fists slide away from our building. The rear fender gleamed when Dad stopped for a red light at the corner, and as he turned there was a flash, like the winking of an eye.

"Yes," I told her, "I can't see him anymore."

"Then that's the last time," she said, moving heavily toward the kitchen.

Dad left on July first. The very next day a heat wave hit Chicago, which seemed associated with the hole in the world Dad left behind. There was an imbalance to things; we had lost our equilibrium and were living at extremes. With a large ice cube in my mouth, I practiced freezing my heart. Mom didn't bother to sit near a fan or wipe the sweat from her forehead with the towel I draped around her neck.

"Are you hungry?" I asked her because I was, and my brothers were chewing on dry cereal while they watched the Three Stooges. She didn't answer or even act as if she heard me. A tear of sweat rolled from her temple to the curve of her jawline, and on down her neck to soak into her red tank top.

"Do you think he'll come back?" I asked her. The fingers of her right hand twitched, but that was her only response.

"C'mon." I herded my brothers into the kitchen and cut them slices of Colby cheese. We ate cheese and buttery Ritz crackers for lunch, and later for dinner.

That week my mother became her own ghost, and I became more real. I learned to heat SpaghettiOs in a pan on the dark metal burners and to light the oven to heat up chicken potpies. At night I wiped my brothers' foreheads with ice wrapped in a washcloth, and made sure the fan was blowing straight onto their small forms. It was a week of heat, quiet, and solitude.

Mom came back to us a little at a time. One night she laughed at something on TV and we all came running to laugh with her. "What is it, Mom, what's so funny?" I sat on the edge of her easy chair and put my arm around her damp shoulder.

"Hmmm?" She peered at the three of us, taking stock, and we moved instinctively closer like wealth to be counted. Billy planted his hands on her knees and rocked toward her face.

"We heard you," he whispered, and then he laughed out loud because she bumped her nose against his. "Eskimo kiss!" Billy shouted.

One week had passed. My brothers found solace in Tonka trucks and a G.I. Joe with a furry crewcut and kung-fu grip. I trailed after my mother, determined to ward off her unhappiness with my vigilance. One evening we sat together. It was later than it looked. We had all the windows pushed open as wide as they would go.

"An inch of breeze is an inch of breeze," Mom had said as we helped her tug on window sashes warped by the heat.

I sat across from Mom at the kitchen table. She was doing

the *TV Guide* crossword puzzle, and I was pretending to color pictures in a coloring book while I was really keeping an eye on her.

"What's the name of that guy from 'Little House on the Prairie'?" she asked me, the tip of her pen waving over the paper.

"Michael Landon," I said. "He played the pa."

That made her look up before she finished writing his name, and she glanced at my artwork. She moved her arms, about to get up from the table, but her skin was warm and stuck to the Formica. My arms were stuck, too, and when I finally pulled them free, they were greasy, coated with toast crumbs.

Mom laughed. "Now you know what a bug stuck to flypaper feels like." Then she cocked her head at the silence. "Say, what are your brothers up to? They've been too quiet." Mom left to find Billy and Grover after wiping her arms with a dishtowel. The kitchen was darker all of a sudden. I could hear cicadas thrumming from the vacant lot next door and I had this sad, loose-ends feeling of wasted time.

Mom came back into the kitchen brandishing her red patent-leather purse. She waved it in the air, saying, "Let's make us some black cows!" So the four of us went to the corner liquor store, where we bought vanilla ice cream, root beer, and striped plastic straws for our floats. But Grover said he wanted his ice cream in Coke, so then Billy wanted Coke, too. Mom made a face but she let them switch their A & W's for Cokes.

On the way back Mom spotted a thick patch of milk-weed as high as her waist in the vacant lot.

"Look at this," she said. She reached out her free hand to gauge the weight of green pods heavy with latex. "Just what you kids need, some green in your diet." Mom handed

me the black cow fixings, starting to break out of the
moist bottom of the paper bag, and put the keys in my
pocket.

"Why don't you run this up before it melts and then
come back? I'm going to collect some of these greens." By
the time I returned it was almost dark and her arms were full
of thick-stemmed milkweeds looking like an exotic bridal
bouquet.

Grover and Billy were picking around by the Dumpster,
so I went to collect them. "Look, Jessie," Grover hissed. He
pulled Billy out of the way so I could see. Some winos were
passed out in the space between the Dumpster and the brick
wall of our building. The smell rising from their niche was
worse than that coming from the open garbage. I couldn't
count how many there were, maybe three or four, because
they were piled in a confusion of dirty clothes, their legs
stacked together like wood.

"Get away from there!" Mom called us back and hefted
the plants higher in her arms. "Leave those poor drunks
alone. Let them sleep it off in peace."

"Are they dead?" Billy asked me as we followed Mom
and the cluster of milk flowers nodding over her shoulder.

"No," I said, "they're just sleeping." I could tell Billy
didn't believe me. I heard him whisper to Grover when we
were walking up the stairs: "Dad wouldn't of left those dead
Indians to get eaten by flies."

We both hushed him.

Dad had been gone exactly two weeks and Mom was
making sounds about the future. She said, "With me going
back to work, you'll have more responsibilities."

Her fingers were smoothing out a white athletic sock,

one of Dad's. She caught me watching her and quickly balled the sock into a tight wad, chucking it basketball-style into the tall kitchen trash can. She pressed her empty hands against the table and smiled. "Everything's going to be okay, though. It'll be all right."

"I know," I told her.

My mother held her arms out to me in a way she hadn't done since I was as young as my brothers. I moved hesitantly, but she pulled me onto her lap and our bare legs, poking out of polyester shorts, slid together like held hands.

"I guess you're not too young for me to talk to real serious."

I couldn't see her; we were both facing the refrigerator door, taped all over with poems cut out of Indian newspapers like *News from Indian Country* and *Akwesasne Notes*. The printing was so small that from across the room it looked like trails of sugar ants crawling up and down. Mom talked over my shoulder, her warm breath sliding past my neck.

"Listen up now," she began, but interrupted herself. She leaned against me to bury her face in my hair. "Boy, it sure smells sweet," Mom said, "and it's real pretty. Always was pretty." I knew she meant my unusual red hair.

"See." She was holding pale strands near the window, where they glistened in the sunlight. "It's just like Black Hills gold. Three different colors woven together." Mom paused, my hair held close to her eyes. She was suddenly very quiet, and I could feel tears gathering in the air.

"I want to tell you something, okay? Just because your father took off on some crazy adventure doesn't mean he stopped caring about us. He's just mixed up. He thinks he's doing the right thing, but he's forgetting that a Sioux man's first duty is to his family." Mom was crying now, her tears falling on my thighs like the first warning drops of rain. "Do you hear me?"

I nodded and swallowed my own throat again and again. *Don't defend him,* I wanted to tell her, but I remained silent. I stroked Mom's hand with my fingers. I was tired of seeing my mother rub away, becoming so thin the few wrinkles on her forehead pulled taut across the bone, her face as smooth as the worry stones I saw between the fingers of old women in Greek Town.

Grandma Mabel came for a visit that summer, smelling faintly of sweet grass. She entered our apartment gracefully. Her ancient carpetbag (which she said dated back to the Truman administration), heavy support hose, and worn bowling sneakers did not detract from her air of dignity.

I meant to give Grandma a tour of our apartment when I took her hand, leading her from room to room. But along the way she took over and began labeling familiar objects. She pointed to my parents' bedside table, its one short leg propped higher with a *Reader's Digest.*

She said, *"Wáglutapi,"* and dropped her hand. Grandma paused, looking at me.

"Wáglutapi?" I repeated. Grandma nodded. She pointed to the door: *"Tiyópa";* the window, *"Ožanžanglépi."* In the kitchen she poked her finger at the dingy stove. *"Očéti,"* she said. Billy had left a soda can on the kitchen table and Grandma snatched it, waving it before my face. *"Kapópapi,"* she told me, wiggling her eyebrows. It had a funny sound. I couldn't say it correctly because each time I tried, I sputtered laughter. Pretty soon the two of us were holding each other for support, Grandma shaking and shaking with light, almost soundless gasps, wafting like smoke rings to the ceiling.

"Oh, I've got to pee," she finally managed, and rushed past me to the bathroom. I'd never seen an old lady move so quickly.

At night the two of us shared my bed, across the room from where my little brothers slept in a tangle of bony elbows. Grandma wore white cotton anklets to bed. "When you get old the blood doesn't reach your feet anymore," she explained. And she never wore a real nightgown. Instead she pulled on one of her old housedresses, worn away almost to gauze, the print on the fabric washed off long ago. She had a set of rosary beads that glowed in the dark. She wore them around her neck and they glared at me like little eyes unless I slept with my back to her.

After saying her prayers in Sioux, she would pull me against her, a heavy arm draped across my waist. The smell of sweet grass was so thick in the bed I imagined we were sleeping on the plains.

It was Grandma Mabel who told me about the roofwalker. "My *tunkášila*, that's my grandfather, first saw the roofwalker standing in the sky, his wings stretched so wide he covered the light of the moon and most of the stars. My *tunkášila* said the roofwalker was born out of misery, right after the Wounded Knee massacre, where so many of our people were killed for holding a Ghost Dance. They were buried in the snow and the roofwalker drifted over their mass grave, his eyes big and hungry, so empty my *tunkášila* hunched in the snow, afraid he would be eaten.

"And now that roofwalker has followed me to Chicago. Isn't he crazy? He'll get lost and never find the Dakotas again. He'll choke over those steel mills or fly straight into that John Hancock Building, won't he?"

Grandma tickled me with her stubby fingers and we almost rolled out of the bed with our giggling. To finish the story, however, Grandma became serious. She whispered as if the roofwalker were listening. I kept glancing at the window, expecting to see the smoky steam of his breath, but the window was clear black.

She told me that the roofwalker was a Sioux spirit, a kind of angel. "He isn't good or bad, though," she said. "He just is."

The roofwalker was the hungriest of all spirits, hugely, endlessly hungry, his stomach an empty cavern of echoes.

"You see," Grandma said, "even though he's starving, he is fussy. Always holding out for a delicacy."

The roofwalker lived to eat dreams, and when he feasted on the dream of his choice, it always came true. "Did he ever get one of yours?" I asked Grandma Mabel, trying to imagine what a dream tasted like, and how you could fit it in your mouth without choking.

"Yes, he did," she said. She smoothed the hair off my forehead. "I dreamed you."

I let my head fall back against Grandma's chest. I could feel her rosary beads tangle in my hair and rub against my scalp. I dreamt that we were sleeping on the prairie, Grandma's finger pointing out the stars, her arms so long she could reach up and dust them.

That fall after Grandma Mabel returned to North Dakota, her voice remained in my head, repeating stories and Sioux vocabulary words. I think that is why the creature came to me. He stepped full-grown from my dreams, a night visitor prowling through my thoughts, and later, quite fleshed out, hovering outside my bedroom window as if treading air. My brothers slept on in the next bed that night. I could see their gray outline and the hang of loose arms, thin as sticks.

I wanted to wake them, to ask them, "Do you see him

out there? Has he gone?" But I didn't. Instead I admired the creature's brown, hairless body, glistening and smooth. He seemed eager, his mouth open and barbed tongue curled over his teeth. His eyes were penetrating, the black pupils drilled; I was convinced he could see right through my brain and spot my dreams. I knew what that tongue was for. I knew what he did. He was a dream eater. The tiny curved thorns lining the edge of his tongue like needles were for catching dreams. His tongue was flexible enough for excavation, like delicate surgery, and after he swallowed an extracted dream, it would come true.

I wasn't surprised that he looked just like my father, although his thick waist-length hair was trimmed with feathers. The handsome face and the strong arms and torso were my father's. Only the legs were different: feathered haunches, and curved talons for feet.

"You are part bird," I whispered to him through the pane of glass separating us. "You are part spirit." His eyes stared without expression, but his hand lifted a necklace worn against his chest, which was strung with bear claws, elk teeth, and rare dentalium shells. I tried to reach my hand through the glass to stroke the necklace he proffered with a graceful hand, but as I grazed the barrier, he flew upward and I heard a backwash of wind forced by the beating of powerful wings.

In the morning I looked for scattered red and black feathers, the colors of his plumage. I couldn't find any, but that didn't shake my faith. I knew the roofwalker had visited me. He was as real as I needed him to be.

When I was little I had blind faith in family legends, my grandmother's stories, and even in my handsome father, who was temporarily lost, searching for the road Grandma

Mabel told me was beneath my own feet. After all, he had been the one to catch me before I slipped to the floor, the one who kept me in the world once my mother released me.

Grandma Mabel told me that life is a circle, and sometimes we coil around on ourselves like a drowsy snake. Weeks after Grandma Mabel returned to North Dakota, I decided to circle back to my own beginning. Perhaps that was where I should go to make things right, to bring my father home to his lonesome family. It seemed very clear to me what I had to do.

It was my tenth birthday. I woke before anyone else and dressed quietly so I wouldn't wake my brothers. I looked out of the front window and watched the leaves fall, tugged loose by a morning wind. I slipped out of the front door but left it unlocked for my return.

I chose the place carefully, somewhere high enough to test faith, but not so high as to be dangerous. I stood at the top of the final flight of stairs leading to our tiled vestibule. I was ten carpeted steps away from the front door of our building. I curled the edges of my feet over the top step, feeling the space slope forward and downward. I lunged chin first into the fall with eyes closed, my body as relaxed as the startled release of tension before sleep. I waited for Dad to catch me, for the roofwalker to throw back his head and open his mouth, letting my dream float up from his throat, into the breeze rolling away from Lake Michigan.

A Loss in Detroit

By *Sharon Dilworth*

The Lions are scheduled to play the Browns at noon. Grandma and I are sitting in front of her big bay window eating white herring snacks on rye crackers. Outside the game traffic moves slowly up the street to the Pontiac Silverdome. From where we are sitting we can also see Grandma's 1972 aqua-blue-body, black-top Chevy Bel-Aire, which is parked at the far end of the carport.

"This time it's the water pump," my grandmother tells me. "I didn't even know a car had a water pump. Did you?"

"No." I shake my head. This is my first family holiday since my divorce, and I am preoccupied by my depression and loneliness. My sadness feels like a heavy snowsuit that I used to wear as a kid, only now there is no one to help me take it off. Aunt Donna is having the turkey dinner at her place later this afternoon, but I am not up to seeing the whole family. There will be too many relatives asking me questions about how I am and how sad it is that this had to happen. And if they're not asking me questions, then I will be angry at their lack of concern.

Grandma snorts at my answer and I tune back into the conversation. "I mean yes. Yes. Of course. All cars have water pumps."

The twins, my twenty-two-year-old cousins, are in charge of fabricating car problems that make it impossible for my grandmother to even consider driving down to the grocery store. They are seniors at the University of Michigan in Ann Arbor, and neither knows the first thing about automobiles.

Born the year the century turned, Grandma is alert, energetic, sharp, and enthusiastic, but she has never been a good driver. The twins come up with excuses to keep her from getting behind the steering wheel. Two months ago, it was a lost gas cap, which Grandma was suspicious about. She called the neighborhood Texaco station and the owner told her to stick a rag in the hole until she could get to K-Mart to buy a new one. The twins told her the guy must have been absolutely nuts to give her that kind of advice.

The family talks about selling the Chevy. This is the year, everyone agrees. It's finally time to get rid of that old thing. They have talked like this for more than a decade.

My father, who was working for General Motors back in 1972, helped my grandparents finance the Bel-Aire. My grandfather wouldn't let anyone drive it. He rarely took it out himself, claiming that people drove without respect on the Detroit highways. Still, every night at dusk, he would go downstairs, brush the Dutch elm leaves off the hood of the car, polish the side-view mirrors with his shirtsleeve, check the head- and taillights. Once inside, he'd roll down the window and begin playing with the lighter. He frequently complained to my father that it was broken and my father would take it over to the Chevy dealer on Vandyke and Five Mile Road, who never found anything wrong with it. My grandfather was an impatient man who couldn't leave the lighter pushed in long enough for the coils to heat up. Frustrated, he'd take a pack of matches from his jacket pocket and light his cigar. Grandpa smoked what my father called OPC—Other People's Cigars. Brand was never important. My father and his brothers had stopped pooling their Detroit Golf Club caddy money to buy him expensive black-market Cuban cigars. Instead, they'd walk over to Varsity Lanes on Livernois and buy him the bowling alley four-for-a-dollar specials.

A Catholic ghetto is what my mother called the neighborhood where I grew up. The homes, two-story postwar structures, were mostly red brick with aluminum siding. Each house had a square front lawn divided by a straight sidewalk running up to the front door. My mother was never as thrilled as I was that my father's entire family lived in a four-block radius. My grandmother lived one block over on Stopel Avenue. A three-family dwelling, it was built in 1907 by her father, a porter for the Book-Cadillac Hotel in downtown Detroit. His wife, hit by a streetcar when she was forty, could not manage the flights of stairs by herself. Worried that she'd fall or hurt herself and not be able to get help, he installed voice tubes in every room. The tubes were built into the thick walls and run from my grandmother's apartment on the top floor to my great-aunts' apartment on the street level. (They are triplets—Faith, Hope, and Charity. My father is Faith's godchild. Every Christmas she sends him a pair of dark-brown corduroy slacks, every birthday a light-blue buttondown.) The voice tubes continue from there to the basement, where various second cousins and nonrelatives board. My parents were always telling us to quit shouting in the walls, but the tubes provided hours of entertainment for me and my cousins whenever we visited Stopel. That's what we called her house. Never Grandmother's or Mother's—it was always Stopel. As in "Easter dinner will be at Stopel this year."

My grandmother, who can remember the lace trim around the collar of her third-grade Communion dress, and the undercooked chicken she was served at the Detroit River restaurant forty-five years ago, doesn't bother to call her grandchildren by their own names. We are grouped according to our parents' names. I am one of Eddie's. My cousin Rita is a Norm. Kathy, Jim, and Mike are Donna's.

My grandfather's funeral was packed with relatives and friends. A line ran from the casket, around the folding chairs, and up to where Grandma stood beside a table that had four photographs of Grandpa. She was in every one of them. There were so many people waiting to console my grandmother that I didn't worry about saying much to her myself. I hugged her and mumbled something about Grandpa. Then I moved to the other side of the room and sat with my cousins, who were tying rubber bands to the bottoms of the folding chairs. I was not in the room when they pulled the chain and made the chairs collapse like dominoes.

Shortly after the funeral, my parents invited my grandmother to dinner and I was mortified. I didn't want to see her. It seemed wrong that she was alive when Grandpa was dead. I told my mother that Rachel Sundquist's mother had invited me for supper. This was a lie. Rachel Sundquist's mother was an emergency-room nurse and she never made dinner. Rachel and her brothers bought things in boxes and heated them up to eat in front of the television. My mother insisted that I stay home. "This is a hard time for your grandmother. She wants you near her."

"Why?" I asked. "Why would she want me around?"

"Be cheerful," my mother advised. "You're a happy person. You can smile and laugh, and that will make her happy."

I waited until I heard Grandma's voice in the front hallway before I got into the shower. I knew they would have cocktails and hors d'oeuvres for at least an hour. Dripping wet, I stood in my towel at the top of the stairs and tried to hear the conversation. I wanted to know what they were talking about. What did someone who has just lost her husband talk about?

My older sister was sent upstairs to tell me that dinner was ready. My mother had put a tablecloth on the dining room table. We would be eating on the good dishes—there was wine and cloth napkins. I became suddenly busy watering the African violets lining my windowsill. I had named each one of them after the characters in the Gothic romances I was reading. That week they were called Heathcliff, Rochester, Catherine. My sister warned me that my mother was impatient with my hiding act, so I went downstairs and walked straight into the kitchen. I asked her what she needed me to do and she told me that my hair was wet. She tucked the long ends into the collar of my shirt, but the dampness was uncomfortable and I flipped it out in one defiant motion.

"At least braid it," she ordered, and handed me a thick

kitchen rubber band. I did it knowing that the hair would tangle when I pulled it loose.

At the dinner table I was seated next to my grandmother. She cried openly as my mother filled her plate with sweet potatoes and thin slices of ham. We talked about the closing of a Catholic church on the west side of the city and how the family was slowly abandoning the city of Detroit. If Grandma realized that my parents were getting ready to sell Stopel and move her to a condominium in the northern suburbs, she didn't let on. The conversation never got around to Grandpa. Grandma blew her nose into her cloth napkin and asked me how school was going. I told her it was fine, but I couldn't think of anything more to say. I didn't feel like being cheerful. A few minutes later she set her napkin on top of her untouched food. This struck me as childish. She acted like she was hiding her food—afraid that someone would punish her for not eating. I was embarrassed by the way she was behaving—so open about her loss. I had heard about people who could not live without their spouses. I wondered if my grandmother would die before the year's end.

I was sixteen when my grandfather died. Early October and I had been driving for three months. It could have been four, but I twice flunked my driver's license test. First there was the problem with the stop sign, then a slight problem with the curb during parallel parking. My parents let me drive the aqua-blue, black-top Chevy Bel-Aire until Grandma got used to the changes in her life. I was grateful for the transportation, but had trouble with the manual brakes and manual steering. My friends had more problems with the smell. They coughed and make gagging noises when I drove them around suburban Detroit. It was the first time I identified the odor with my grandfather. The car reeked of his cigars. I dumped the ashtray out on the school parking lot. There were no butts, but a few ashes flew into the wind.

Twenty years later the car still smells of my grandfather's cigars. It's best to drive with the windows rolled down even in the dead of winter. My mother, who had the car for seven weeks when Grandma and her Mature Minglers group was touring the Alaska coastline, took it to Jax's on Woodward and asked that they do a special inside wash with deodorant. They hung a Christmas tree from the rearview mirror, which filtered the scent of evergreen. None of this was strong enough to kill the everlasting odor of my grandfather's cigars.

My grandmother dismisses any talk of selling the Chevy.

"Nonsense," she tells her children. "I can't live in suburban Detroit without a car. No one lives in Detroit without a car."

"We'll make sure you get where you have to go," Donna assures her. "We're always here for you."

"I prefer to be independent," Grandma says.

My grandmother is unfazed by things the family thinks will upset her—my father's two heart attacks, Matt's incarceration and later escape from the state prison, an illegitimate great-grandchild by her sixteen-year-old grandchild. She gets unnerved by babies crying at the overcrowded

Christmas Eve Mass, or losing one of her dime-store clip-on earrings, or when I buy her 7-Up instead of Diet Sprite. "I wouldn't dream of asking you to go back to the store, but I'm afraid those cans of soda pop will just sit in the back of my refrigerator until doomsday. Unless, of course, they explode first."

After an eighteen-month separation, my husband and I are finally divorced. I did not want the marriage to end and am stubborn about signing the final papers. I wait until it is final before telling my family. Certainly they know Jack and I are having problems, but I keep the finality of the situation from them. It's not because the majority of my relatives are still practicing Catholics, as most of my friends thought, but because I am embarrassed to admit that I have failed. I am also suspicious that my relatives prefer Jack to me and that my solo visits to their parties and holiday get-togethers will disappoint them.

Though I dreaded her knowing most, Grandma is the first to call.

"I just can't believe it," she says. It takes me a minute to recognize her voice. Grandma is not a big phone person. She usually sends note cards with her initial on the faint pink paper. The address is never quite correct—a mixture of my home and work. They arrive weeks after she mails them.

Now she tells me how much she has always loved Jack. We belong together, she insists. She is praying for a happy ending to all this.

"You should have stayed with Peter," Grandma says just before she hangs up. "He didn't seem like the kind of man who would get divorced."

"I never dated any Peter," I tell her. I am impatient to end the conversation. "You must be mixing me up with Susie or Rita."

"No. It was you."

The day after my divorce was finalized, I wrote down the names of all the guys I had dated. It didn't take me very long. Jack and I have been together more or less since high school. There weren't very many names on the list, I decided. Not nearly enough for someone my age.

"I don't know any Peters," I say. "I've never known a Peter."

"Sure you do." She is firm. "His mother was Swedish. His father worked for some bottling company downriver. Wyandotte. Maybe Inkster. He had a brother on the track team."

I haven't the slightest idea who she's talking about, but then a name slips off my tongue. "Peter Albright?" I ask. Peter Albright sat across from me in some class when I was a sophomore.

"Right," she says. "Peter. Remember Peter?"

"Not really," I say, and then ask, "Why are we talking about Peter?" Peter and I had gone on one or two ice-skating dates at Eaton Park. Grandma must have been at the house when he came by to get me. I don't remember them talking. They could only have exchanged a few words while I went downstairs to get my ice skates. She is someone who has problems remembering my first name. I don't know how she can remember Peter Albright—someone I have not thought of since the tenth grade. More important, I want to know why she is bringing him up. Why now?

Thanksgiving Day, and the Lions have lost the coin toss. The Browns go for the kickoff. Traffic has all but disappeared. I eat one more cracker—the white herring is gone—and then stand to go. Grandma suggests we watch a bit more of the game. Neither one of us cares who wins, but my father has bought tickets again this year and ten or twelve of my cousins are there. They will be sitting in the very top rows, nosebleed country, but the cameras sometimes pan that far north.

"You doing okay?" Grandma asks, and I know she is asking about my husband. I am so tired of being sad, but more tired of pretending that I am fine. I tell her that it's not getting any better. I miss him. This isn't changing.

"You'll probably miss him for the rest of your life," she tells me, and I groan.

"Ed's been dead almost twenty years. I didn't think I'd make it through the first night."

The morning sky, full of a gray light, has moved west. It is now a typical November day in Detroit; the room is full of shadows. I can't see her face. Everyone has told me that it gets easier with time. They tell me that I will meet someone new, that the pain will ease, that I'll forget about Jack. One day he will call and I'll have to ask who it is. Grandma disagrees.

"Maybe that happens to some people," she says. "But I don't know. Just because you lose something doesn't mean you forget it."

"I don't think I can live like this," I say. I know it sounds full of self-pity, but I want somebody to tell me something that will help the nights get better. I can't stand waking up at four or five in the morning. The room is dark. I'm alone and don't see anything changing. I am almost certain that I am going to be alone for the rest of my life and I can't bear it. "I don't want to live."

"Oh, you'll live all right," she tells me. "There's no question about that. You will live."

Grandma gets up and I follow her into the kitchen. She opens a can of tuna fish. I cut up sweet dill pickles and celery and we mix in mayonnaise and mustard and then spread our salad on white toast. If I go to Donna's turkey dinner, I will not be hungry.

"I think if I could do it all over again, I would have married someone who was going to live longer," Grandma says. She carefully slices off the crusts and hands me my plate.

"Grandpa lived a long time," I say.

"I know," she says, and then laughs. "It's so silly. I know I can't change anything, but sometimes I think I wish he would have lived just a bit longer."

Grandma cuts the crusts off the bread and then adds a sprig of parsley to each of our plates. She pours white wine into orange juice tumblers. It tastes like the inside of her refrigerator.

"It's like you wishing you had married Peter instead of Jack," she says, and I don't remind her that *she* was the one who came up with this regret. "Peter might still be around," she says. "It's no fun being alone. No matter what people tell you—it never gets to be any fun."

We eat lunch in front of the television. They don't show much of the fans, but every once in a while they pan the audience, showing someone waving an oversized Styrofoam finger or someone who has painted his face silver and blue. By halftime, worn out from crying, I fall asleep. Grandma covers me with the afghan I made her, the only thing I've ever crocheted. I sleep a couple of hours, and when I wake, she's getting ready to take her bath. The Browns have won and the Silverdome is clearing out quickly and I rush outside in an attempt to beat the exiting traffic. I'm too late. The street is once again blocked by the slow-moving cars—one continuous line of traffic. It will be an hour before I can make a left-hand turn onto Opdyke Road to get to my parents' house. My grandmother must be napping or running the water for her bath. She doesn't answer the bell. I stand on the sidewalk and watch the gray sky spit rain and snowflakes into the shadowy day.

The Chevy sits in Grandma's carport. The odor of my grandfather's cigars is just as fresh as it was when he was alive. I can imagine him putting one out in the crowded ashtray, then going upstairs to be with my grandmother one more night. My grandmother has not driven the car in years. There is no danger that she will drive it anytime soon. She probably knows she will never drive it. But it is hers and this is where it belongs.

I have fifty-eight more years to go before I turn ninety-two. The year will be 2050.

Grandma

By Erin Khue Ninh

My mother once told me the story of Grandma's life. She was born on a large farm, the eldest daughter in a family full of girls. Grandma's mother died when Grandma was twelve, so the farm, and everyone on it, became her responsibility. She worked the rice paddies and reared her younger sisters, took care of her father, sewed the family's clothes, and cared for an attic full of silkworms. I remember Grandma telling me how the sticky multitudes of tiny, filmy mounds clung to the screens. How she'd dip the screens into boiling water to kill the worms, then unravel each cocoon from a single strand of silk.

In what time she had, she learned to read. Never to write. One of her uncles taught her; girls weren't allowed to go to school then. She still sounds words out, slowly, in a strange singsong kind of chant like that of Buddhist monks at temple, whether it's a letter she's reading or "kinh."*

When she was nineteen or so, she got married. She wasn't a very pretty girl—dull featured and rough palmed. But it was a marriage of love.

* praying

Her two little boys died in infancy. And then her husband. She returned to her father's house. At twenty-nine, she married again. My grandfather was fifty-three at the time, a famous Chinese herbal-medicine man. People came to him from all over Vietnam to be cured of cancer and other terminal diseases. His first wife had passed away; he wanted someone to take care of the house and of his youngest daughter. His other children were grown, the eldest but a few years younger than my grandmother. And they did not like this country woman. They determined that she would not forget her place: second wife, and not much more than a servant one hired for free. My mother remembers nights when Grandma would sit on their bed in a room dark with the shadows of a single kerosene lamp, holding her little girl in her arms and rocking back and forth, back and forth, weeping, weeping. Grandfather didn't stop his children from being cruel to Grandma, but he never was. And he adored my mother, his youngest child by far, the one of his old age. She was Grandma's last child, and the only one to live. My grandmother had miscarried or buried three more babies before her—all boy children. It was in Grandma's "so," her fate, they'd always said, that she could raise no boys. But her little girl grew up determined to succeed, to show them all, to bring her mother honor. My mother brought Grandma out, all the way to America.

But the story does not end there. Grandma is eighty-six now. She loves us dearly, my sister and me, and has gotten better at showing it through the years. Every so often, she will reach up for a clumsy kiss, unpracticed, like a child's. She never kissed my mother. She showed that she cared by yelling at her, cursing her. *I would not hurt you if I did not love you.* To this day my mother cannot bring herself to give my grandmother a kiss, as much as she wants to.

I have known a little of that harsh affection. When I was four or five, Grandma yelled at me until I learned to read Vietnamese. When she used to give me a bath, she'd scrub me till it hurt and grip my arm so tightly, I thought she was afraid I'd run away. I give *her* a bath now. She hasn't anyone to teach anymore, no silkworms to care for, no one to tend to. Her biggest concern nowadays is finding the scissors we always misplace so she can cut the napkins in two—using the whole napkin is wasteful. She shuffles in, shuffles out, with no one to talk to, nothing to do. And her eyes are failing, so her sole occupation, her "kinh," is failing her.

Grandma lives with us, in a world all her own. She tells stories no one hears—we block them out, having heard them too many times before. It's as though she's worn grooves into her mind for certain words, phrases, stories, and these are perforce the only path the cart's wheels will follow. The rest of the ground has slowly fallen away, disintegrated through disuse—and slowly continues to do so. We ignore her guiltily, knowing we have nothing to say, fearing to speak lest we get her started, knowing the conversation would only end in anger and frustration. Her words are like raindrops, harmless, but falling relentlessly on a single spot, making it sensitive and sore.

There it is. No tale of redemption, of struggle and triumph. It started a long time ago, in a land far, far away, and that's as much of the fairy tale as you'll get from me. There is but one end to this story, and its happiness lies in that it is wished for. Take it as you will. I think it's a damn sad story.

The Magical Grandmother

By *Maxine Hong Kingston*

Grandfather, Ah Goong, plowed fields hour after hour alone, inching along between earth and sky. To amuse himself, he sang girls' songs in an old man's falsetto. He wished for a happy daughter he could anticipate seeing in the evenings after work; she would sing for him and listen to him sing. He tied his ox near some water and took a walk about the village to find out what the neighbors were doing. One family he often visited had had a baby due at the same time as our family. After seeing what he himself had gotten, he went to find out what they'd gotten. His mouth and throat, his skin puckered all over with envy. He discovered why to be envious is "to guzzle vinegar." Theirs was the loveliest dainty of a baby girl. She lay ignored in a yam basket. He gazed at her and sang to her until he had to leave, should he fall farther behind in his plowing. The next time he visited, he brought her a red ribbon, which he fashioned into a bow and arranged by her ear. He laughed at the air it gave her. She wore rags, which sent waves of delicious pity coursing through him. "Poor girl," he said. "Poor, poor girl."

The day his third son stomped on the baby, Ah Goong sneaked away from the commotion. He scooped up party food on the way out. He went to the girl's house. He tucked red packets of money in her faded shirt, no special red dress for her today, no new red jacket, no tiger shoes nor hat with eight boy dolls for tassels. Her family offered him shredded carrots, scant celebration. How sorry he felt for her, how he loved her. She cried, squeezing bitty tears out of her shut lids. His heart and his liver filled with baby tears. Love filled his heart and his liver. He piled grapefruits and oranges in a pyramid for her. He tarried so long that he had to use the outhouse, but he carefully weighed his shit on the outhouse scales so that these neighbors could return a like amount to his fields.

He cut a reed from the New Year narcissus and blew tunes between his thumbs. Though the snowpeas would be fewer at harvest, he brought the girl their blossoms, pinks with purple centers, light blues with dark blue centers, the vine flowering variously as if with colors of different species. She chewed on the flowers and pulled the tendrils apart in her chubby hands. Extravagance. In the summer he fanned her with a sandalwood fan; he rubbed its ribs with sandpaper, and with one pass, the air thickened with memories of Hawai'i, which is the Sandalwood Mountains. In the autumn the two of them would rattle dry peapods.

"It's only a girl," her parents kept saying. "Just a girl."

"Yes," said Ah Goong. "Pretty little sister. Pretty miss."

Away from her he detached a fuzzy green melon from its nest and tucked it for a moment inside his sweater next to his heart. Whenever he had to leave her, he felt the time until he would see her again extend like an unplowed field, the sun going down and a long country night to come. No, he would not endure it.

He went home and put on the brown greatcoat that he had bought in San Francisco. "Where are you going with that coat in this weather?" asked Ah Po, who did not follow him about the house because of her bound feet; the three maids who fanned her and helped her walk were working in the kitchen. When she walked unassisted or with one maid, she touched the walls gracefully with thumb and little finger spread, index and middle fingers together, fourth finger down. "I'll just take a peek at the baby," he said, "then go out." He picked up his wife's baby and hid him inside his greatcoat. If you had been a little older, BaBa, you might have felt proud, singled out for an excursion that made Ah Goong dance down the road, a bright idea in his head.

He ran into the neighbor's house and unwrapped the baby, first the greatcoat, then the diapers to show the family that this doggy really was a boy. "Since you want a boy and I want a girl," he said, "let's strike a bargain. Let's trade." The family was astounded. They would have let him buy the girl if only he'd asked. They would have had to give her away eventually anyhow. And here was this insane man who did not know the value of what he had. What a senile fool. Take him up on it before he comes to his senses. As if his son's boyness were not enough, he pointed out his attributes. "This boy will be very intelligent," he said. "He's got scholar's hands. And look what a smart forehead he has. He'll win a name for you at the Imperial Examinations. He's very skinny and eats hardly any food."

"Yes, we'll take him," said the neighbors. Ah Goong placed the girl inside his greatcoat. He did not remove the boy's fancy clothes, the gold necklace, the new shoes, nor the jade bracelet that signified that you would not have to do physical labor. He hurried out before her family could change their minds. His heart beat that they would reclaim her at the last minute. The girl wore no jewelry, but with his soul he adopted her, full diapers and all.

He walked slowly, adoring the peachy face. He sat by the side of the road to look at her. He counted her pink toes and promised that no one would break them. He tickled her under the chin. She would make his somber sons laugh. Kindness would soon soften the sides of their mouths. They would kneel to listen to her funny requests. They would beguile her with toys they'd make out of feathers and wood. "I'll make you a doll," he promised her. "I'll buy you a doll." And surely his wife would get used to her soon. The walk home was the nicest time. He showed her, his daughter, how the decorative plants grow wild and the useful plants in rows. "Flower," he said, pointing. "Tree." He rested by the stream for her to listen to its running.

At home, he walked directly to the crib and tucked her in. He drew the quilt over her as a disguise. Then he hung up his greatcoat and returned to the crib, gave the quilt a pat. She was a well-behaved baby and made no noise. He kept strolling past the crib. His happiness increased in her vicinity. "My heart and my liver," he called her. (*Sweetheart* is an English word that emigrants readily learn.)

Ah Po heard the sniffing and squeaking of a baby waking up. She swayed over to the crib. The baby noises sounded unfamiliar. She screamed when she saw the exchanged baby.

Ah Goong came running. "What's wrong? What's wrong?" he asked.

"What is this? Where's my baby?" Ah Po yelled.

"It's all right." He patted the baby. "Everything's all right. He's at the neighbors'. They'll take good care of him."

"What neighbors?" she yelled. "What's he doing at the neighbors'? Whose is this ugly thing?"

"Oh, no, she isn't ugly. Look at her." He picked her up.

"Where's my baby? You crazy old man. You're insane. You idiot. You dead man."

"The neighbors have him. I brought this one back in his place." He held his little girl. "All we have are boys. We need a girl."

"You traded our son for a girl? How could you? Who has my son? Oh, it's too late. It's too late." She thrust her arms as far as she could reach; she bent her torso from side to side, backward and forward, a woman six feet tall on toy feet. "Take me to that family," she cried. "We're trading back." Lunging her weight at Ah Goong, who hunched his shoulders and caved in his chest to protect the baby, she pushed him out the door. She walked in back of him, shoving him while hanging on to his shoulder. She was not used to dashing about on the roads. "I'm coming to rescue you, BiBi. Your mother's coming." Ah Goong clung to his baby as if she were holding him up. "Dead man," Ah Po raged, "trading a son for a slave. Idiot." He led her to the neighbors' house, weeping as he walked. "Dead demon." The villagers lined the road to look at Grandfather and Grandmother making fools of themselves.

Ah Po scolded the girl's family. "Cheating the greedy pig, huh? Thieves. Swindlers. Taking advantage of an idiot. Cheaters. Trying to catch a pig, are you? Did you really think you'd get away with it? Pig catchers. A girl for a boy. A girl for a boy." The family hung their heads.

She pulled the girl out of Ah Goong's arms and shoved her at an older child. Her own baby she snatched and held tight. She sent for her sedan chair and waited for it in the road. She carried her son herself all the way home, not letting Ah Goong touch her baby, not letting him ride. He hardly saw the road for his tears. Poor man.

Telling Tales and Mississippi Sunsets

⌒⌒

By Gloria Naylor

It is summer in Harlem. And the women are old. Friends.
Callie Canada has come to visit Luceilia Johnson. Callie
now lives in Chicago among numberless grandchildren.
Luceila owns a battered tenement with apartments that has
housed over the years many of her own children—and
numberless grandchildren. Miss Callie and Miss Ceil. Both
women are widows. Both find little need for talk that will
fill in the empty spaces for me between the mention of a
name and laughter, a name and raised eyebrows, a name—
and silence: "Where *is* he now?" while as a child I hunger
for the then.

I had the two grandmothers for the price of one heritage:
my parents grew up next to each other in a small settlement
of sharecroppers in Robinsonville, Mississippi. I must flesh
out these women from stories handed down to me from the
two camps of in-laws, two sets of aunts and uncles who

grew up together. "Miss Ceil was something else." And
that's what interests me, the something else, the spaces that
fill in the silence where most of life is lived.

> "When Miss Callie heard that Alberta was going to
> marry your father, she called her over to the house and
> said, Don't you take no junk from him, these Naylor
> men can hand out plenty of junk. And Miss Callie knew
> what she was talking about. She had taken her shotgun
> out a few times over some young girl and Mr. Naylor."

Is it true? I ask the winter shadows that move along the
tar surface of Highway 61 as I make my way toward what
was once Robinsonville, Mississippi. I drive and look for
the ghost of Callie Canada racing through the endless rows
of cotton, the weight of the gun handle pressed under her
right arm, against the side of her breast. Would she kill for a
man? Was she so bad a shot that she kept missing Henry
Naylor and the anonymous paramour over and over again?
Is it true? A senseless question that is answered by the empty
landscape.

> "Miss Ceil never much stayed in that house. She loved to
> go fishing. The only time you'd catch her home was
> when the blacksmith was visiting. The blacksmith was
> always over to their house. And I don't know if Mr.
> Evans minded or not. They sure didn't have a horse."

Robinsonville is a weary cluster of L-shaped stores
hemmed in by a cross section of dry, dusty roads. The dirt
roads lead to dirt fields. The dirt fields lead to the horizon. I
imagine it young and vibrant. I imagine it hot. The sweat
running down the exposed biceps of the man who shaped
iron. Can I see Lueceila Johnson straining up to meet the

body of such a man? Would she do such a thing? No answer from the gray wind that stirs the dust around my ankles. Perhaps I am not asking the right questions.

Callie Canada, why did you marry Henry Naylor?

Girl, do you know what it's like when the sun sets in Mississippi?

Callie Canada, some say he meant more to you than your children.

He meant more to me than my life.

Why?

Watch the sun set in Mississippi.

I walk down a narrow road between the deep ruts left by tractor tires. The few existing houses are wooden shacks, and most of the porches lean. I can tell that these porches have always leaned. They have the look of having been built leaning, and built of weather-worn wood. The people who still hold on in Robinsonville are there because they can't think of anywhere else to call home. Age does this to some. But I wonder about the others. Memphis is only twenty-nine miles north on Highway 61. Less than an hour's drive. I look into the faces of the young and realize that an hour can be too much. There is little for them to do now with machines taking the place of the work that was once done by hand. So much work.

Luecelia Johnson, did you love the gentle Evans McAlpin?

I gave him ten children. Two died.

Luecelia Johnson, some say they weren't all his.

I gave him ten children. Two died.

And so you think you were a good wife?

Girl, watch the sun set in Mississippi.

I do. And it is uneventful. Because the air is so clear around this backwater, there is little to obscure the fact that the sun simply fades below the horizon. The usual reds. The usual purples and deep blues. The last thing to be seen is the endless dirt line along the horizon. I imagine that dirt line full of cotton. I imagine the sun rising on that same dirt line full of cotton. I imagine the sun setting. The sun rising. The sun setting.

When I leave Robinsonville, I sit down at my desk and turn that place into something that it is not. And I invent grand, grand mothers from the spirits of the young women who spoke to me there. But they deserve more than the embellishments of my imagination—or the imaginations of anyone else in our families. The McAlpins and Naylors have, all in our own way, been tellers of tales. The one time I can remember these two women together in the same room the air was heavy and sweet with silence. I will let that silence hold. *This* is only a memorial to all that must be done within the too short hours of darkness in a Mississippi night.

My Grandmothers

By *Mildred Bollinger Andrews*

I am lucky to remember three grandmothers—and have stories of a fourth. I knew my father's mother, my mother's mother, and my mother's grandmother, and I knew of my mother's great-great-great-grandmother, Grandma Hager.

I come from a people who live a long time. Grandma Hager lived to be a hundred and six. This English-German woman was born right before the Revolutionary War, and she lived through the Revolution as a child and on through the War Between the States into Reconstruction days. I'm not sure exactly when Grandma Hager died, but it was before my mother was born, which was in 1881. Grandma Hager was well known, and she was honored by all those who knew her. Married at age thirty-five to a widower with nine children, she was also the mother of nine children. When her last child was born, she was past fifty. Grandma Hager was the mother of my mother's great-great-grandmother, Martha (or Mattie) Bollinger.

Mattie Bollinger lived with her husband and two children, a son and a daughter, in Catawba County, North Carolina. Both her husband and the overseer of his farm, a man who was also the father of two children, fought in the War Between the States. Granny told me war stories— about how they had to eat anything they could get and how they buried food and their silver and any other things they valued in order to hide them.

Grandpa Bollinger and his overseer were both killed in the Battle of Antietam, in Maryland. The men's bodies were brought back across the Potomac to Virginia and buried, and cannons were run over their graves to hide them so the Yankees couldn't dig them up. After the war Granny's neighbors and some soldiers who knew where the men had been buried went back, but they could never find the bodies. Granny was always very upset about not getting her husband's body back. And she never remarried.

Granny was left to bring up her own children and the overseer's children, too. The field slaves left, but the house slaves stayed with Granny and helped her work on the farm, though some of the land had to be sold to pay the heavy taxes that were levied on the South after the war. All four of the children Granny raised turned out well. The overseer's daughter became a designer of dresses, and his son a well-known businessman. Grandma's own son, George, was a civil engineer. He planned routes for railroads that were being built at that time. Her daughter, another Martha, who was called Mat, married a Mr. Burch and eventually gave birth to my mother, Mary Estelle.

Granny was loving and kind. When she visited us in our home, I always slept with her. She wanted me to tell her stories then because she was interested in what I had learned. So I told her about what I had read and been taught, and she listened patiently. In turn, Granny told me her war stories, including what she knew about the Battle of Antietam, when Grandpa was killed. This was one of the bloodiest one-day battles during the war. Her stories gave me a great love for history, especially of the War Between the States. I remember Granny, too, in a wheelchair after she'd had a stroke. She always wanted to be clean. "Hurry up, Mat, and bathe me," she'd say to her daughter. "I want to be clean when I die."

With Grandma Mat, my mother's mother, everything had to be just so—not that we always obeyed her. She begged me and my four sisters never to chew chewing gum because it was not ladylike. She had a strict dress code and was particularly opposed to children wearing socks. Children's legs should be covered with hose held up by garters, according to my grandma.

Grandma Mat wore a lot of black herself, and she wasn't in mourning, either. Grandpa was very much alive. He had been a teacher, and he was quite a wit, always telling jokes and asking us to do silly things. "Get up and move the stove," he once instructed us. "It's getting too hot!" Grandma wouldn't pay any attention to him. She'd lived with him too long, and she was very serious.

But Grandma Mat loved flowers, and she was always giving me plants and cuttings, even when I was very small. There were red peonies in her garden on either side of the gate. Even in her vegetable garden all kinds of flowers grew. The garden was planted in beds with walkways between them, and it was fenced in with a picket fence. A bush grew near one of the windows of Grandma's house, and I could smell it from the window. I don't know its name, but I still remember the scent—it was so wonderful! Once at Duke University I spotted some of those bushes, and their smell brought back memories of Grandma.

Plants weren't all that Grandma Mat gave me. Once she gave me some pigeons and another time a large rag doll named Sally, who was one of my favorites. She sewed well, so she also made me many dresses. As I was the oldest grandchild, perhaps I was Grandma Mat's favorite. I don't remember her ever criticizing me. But that wasn't true for all of us Bollinger girls.

Recently I talked to my sister Ruth about Grandma, and she told me that when she was about four she had scratched Grandma Mat's face out of a family picture with a pin. She was angry with Grandma because Grandma criticized her for the length of her dress and for wearing socks. We'd all seen the picture with Grandma Mat's face scratched out, but nobody knew how it had happened. Ruth never told a soul all those years.

I don't remember as much about my father's mother, Laura Holder Bollinger. I was quite young when she passed away during an epidemic of typhoid fever. She herself wasn't very old when she died, though by then she was a widow who had been left with seven children to raise. I do know that Grandma Bollinger planted her garden in beds like Grandma Mat did. My father told me how he had to weed those beds, and how he hated it. And Grandma gave me a duck once, but it bit and frightened me. I never liked ducks afterward, except in the pond.

After Grandma Bollinger died, my father brought his two younger brothers, whom he always called "the little boys," to our house to live. They remained with us until they married. It seemed when I was growing up that we always had different family members living with us. I don't remember it just being our family in our house till many years later.

Grandmothers are the ones children go to for love, for stories, for comfort when they've been scolded, for guidance, and, of course, for treats. I'm lucky to have known or known about so many of my grandmothers.

Going to Krogers

By Nance Van Winckel

As soon as I get behind the wheel
Gran's saying what to touch
and where to look next. She's blind
and I'm twelve, but this
is an emergency. I back the Studebaker
over the curb, and into a street
not yet wholly familiar.

The trees that line up on the road
seem so newly sketched there
someone could easily come by
and rub them out with a flick
of the wrist. Gran says to stop
at the end of this block. Now what
do I see? Only a parade of cars
with their lights on, though it's
the middle of an afternoon. I sit tall,

as tall as possible, listening hard
to get this, her story of what makes them
follow the dead around like that.
No one looks my way. No one sees

who sits so well under the big wheel.
They stay close on their leader,
taking turns turning in
under the stony-eyed angel.

Trees, and more trees—they keep snapping,
and *what* trees, Gran wants to know.
They bend down and rise up again,
making everything different. Curbed.
Too loud and too many questions.
Will everyone fit at her table?
I can't go any slower, I say,

though the truth was I could.
It was all downhill. She wants
to know each house we've passed,
and she's only brought two dollars
for the butter. I'm all she's got
to help her, she says, just this once
and never let's speak of it again.
Though it's not like anyone expects us
soon. We have hours to kill—

and all she thinks about is her rolls,
for which she believes she is loved.
She's got a hundred things to do, she says,
but she's only named three or four
when I see we've gone too far: the traffic light
comes from nowhere to stop me, though I think

I could figure this out too
if I didn't have to invent yet another
false picture of what's out there.

What's all that noise, she's got to know,
while I'm deciding fast how to turn us
back from the dizzying stream of traffic,
and my stars, she says, now you've
done it. We're out here on the Avenue.

PART TWO

"Put Me Down Easy, Janie,
Ah'm a Cracked Plate."

—ZORA NEALE HURSTON

Seeking Polly, Pretty Polly, Poor Polly, or The Granddaughter Seeks to Remember What the Grandfathers Sought to Forget

⚬⚬

By Daryl Cumber Dance

My great-great-great-grandmother is so special to me because I *found* her despite the fact that she was deliberately written out of my *his*-tory. And this is the story of our meeting.

I grew up in a family and a community that was proud of and protected its heritage. We all felt very special because we were of the lineage of Abraham, our founding father, whose legacy we believed was no less honorable, glorious, and praiseworthy than that of the biblical patriarch whose name he shared. The figure of this venerable forebear, whose legendary deeds were common knowledge, loomed as a prominent force and presence in our daily lives. His achievements and his deeds were recorded in our church history and maintained by family griots. His descendants were traced through the years, and their accomplishments duly noted, so that I could *proudly* trace my line to Abraham and his wife, Susanna—with but one problem. In writing the history, I found out that Abraham left three sons. I later found out about a grandson, Crawford—but Crawford was never listed as one of the sons of Abraham's sons. Whence came Crawford, my great-great-grandfather? Where was the missing link so patently dropped? I wanted to know. How could I complete the chain that ties me to Abraham? As a young person, I asked this obvious question of all the usually talkative family griots, including my maternal grandmother, Sally Carter Brown Bell Brown. All anyone "knew" was that Crawford was Abraham's grandson. When as a slightly more mature young woman, having just finished college in 1958, I pressed one of my elderly great-aunts for information, she finally mumbled something about "having heard the name . . . Polly," but she was so tentative and so uncomfortable talking about it that I knew she wouldn't "know" any more, so I did not pursue the question further.

Over the next thirty years, I didn't get much chance to check on Polly—I was too busy giving her great-great-great-greats, but finally I did get to explore the surviving Charles City County, Virginia, records—deeds, wills, birth and death records, marriage records, court records, etc.—and Polly's name began to turn up, clearly confirming that my great-great-grandfather Crawford had one parent, if not two. First I found Abraham's will and other records of free Negroes that indicated that Abraham and his wife, Susanna, had *several* children other than the three I knew about, including Polly (I expect the achievements of these others were not deemed significant enough to merit inclusion).

But, most important, there *was* a Polly to be deciphered from the reels and reams of insensitive, unfriendly, unwieldy, and sometimes unreadable and untrustworthy county records. Born in 1800, she enjoyed a more privileged life than many of her fellow African-Americans. She was the daughter of a free, property-holding family, having in its household upon Abraham's death china and silver, farm equipment, a spinning wheel, a desk and books. She undoubtedly attended worship services each Sunday at the Elam Baptist Church, which her father and other family members founded in 1810 and which was built on land ceded by Abraham and his wife, Susanna. There she, other free Negroes, and slaves listened to sermons preached by the colored members, as their figurehead white minister (required by the laws of the time) merely came, sat in the most comfortable seat to be had, listened to sermons by some of the colored brothers, drew his one dollar for his attendance, enjoyed a good dinner . . . and quietly sauntered back to his feudal home. He rarely undertook to preach a sermon, but whenever he did, he always preached from one text and only one, which was: "Servants obey your masters." Polly may well have had a little education, since there are indications that members of the family attended their own school until the 1831 law made that illegal.

When she was twenty-one or twenty-three (records conflict), Polly gave birth to the first of her three children, possibly the second of whom was my grandfather Crawford. She is the only parent listed on the birth records located. Having found no record of a father to these children, I expect they were born out of wedlock, *which is probably the reason that she was never mentioned in the family.* Recorded family history notes that Crawford was "born at the old homestead of his grandfather, Abraham Brown," and it appears that Polly continued living on property she inherited from her father. The only other records (save one) that I have found dealing with her are records of sales of land, none of which mentions a husband. They do reveal, however, that she did quite a bit of wheeling and dealing in land for a single woman of her day.

Fascinated by this enigmatic link in the chain of my family tree, I went back to family members, hoping that the *facts* that I could provide them might stimulate them to share with me anything they knew about the family but might be concealing. One cousin, Evalyn Shaed, mentioned to me that she had heard that Polly married her cousin Timothy, but I found nothing to substantiate any marriage. Another cousin who finally acknowledged even knowing the name of Polly was Juanita Carter, who vaguely remembered some tales her mother had told her of "Grandma Polly": she was so beautiful that they had to hide her when the Confederates came through; some of the troops had seen her, and the family had to conceal her to protect her from them (obviously apocryphal since Grandma Polly at sixty probably wouldn't have been such a tempting morsel, though the story might well have grown out of some incident involving troops of some other variety in the county). I uncovered a couple of insinuations that her children were fathered by a prominent white "gentleman" rumored to have begat a number of children by colored women, but the only documented link of any kind between him and this family was the sale of land by him and his wife to Polly's two sons in 1852. While I planned to seek further to find the father of her children, for the moment I was more interested in the life of this newly discovered grandmother.

In addition to the disparagement Polly would have suffered within her family for her illegitimate children, she undoubtedly faced all of the other hardships and restrictions endured by free antebellum blacks during the first half of the nineteenth century, including the indignation of periodically registering and obtaining documentation of her status—which is how I happened to experience the one and only "meeting" with my grandmother.

One day in the mid-1980s, as I sat in the Virginia State Library Archives Room, carefully and cautiously turning the pages of the dusty and crumbling *Register of Free Negroes and Mulattoes, Charles City County,* for 1819, I came across the entry "Polly (daughter of Abram) bright mulatto . . . [has] a scar on left hand . . . small mole to left of nose . . . 5'2½" tall." POLLY . . . Pretty Polly, with a scar on her left hand just *like me—and* a mole *right in the place where mine is*! . . . Polly . . . Poor Polly, who had been lined up on January 24, 1819, before this very book that I sat there holding in my hands more than one hundred and sixty years later! And the only picture that I would ever have of her was this description by a registrar, one of a group of whites not noted for the most sensitive depiction of colored people, but charged to observe those characteristics that might be critical to identification if that was necessary. I'm sure Polly wasn't too comfortable under the gaze of an examiner seeking identifying marks and calling for the requisite information—but what an irony that this ordeal required by her society in order to protect itself from the diminutive twenty-year-old remains as the one physical bond between my great-great-great-grandmother and me! I sat riveted in the Virginia State Archives Room on that day, holding on to that dusty volume as if I were embracing Polly's body, staring at the entry over and over, my imagination admittedly running wild, conjuring up the range of emotions she must have felt at the moment when that entry was recorded, and thrilling at the sense that I had truly recovered her. I had found Polly, truly *found* her. I remained there, enthralled and motionless, fearing that if I moved, if I breathed deeply, I risked losing the spiritual connection that I perceived with her—because I *did* experience a very real sense of her presence; I did know that with the *Register* and me there hovered a once-restless soul, now relieved and peaceful. I felt confident that she would be restored to her rightful place in a line of honored and revered forefathers and mothers.

Ba-Chan

By Anna Esaki-Smith

The good grandmother, my mother's mother, I called White-Haired Ba-Chan. It wasn't until much later that I learned her name was Emi. She played tennis wearing a lightweight kimono and had long white hair, which was always coiled into a deceivingly small bun. Early one morning a few years ago, I peered into her room and saw her kneeling in front of a mirror set atop a low table, combing her hair with a large wooden comb. Her hair looked clean and oiled, but no longer truly white as it did outside against the trees and sky. Wire hairpins were scattered in her lap. She appeared almost girlish with hair draping both sides of her face, falling well below her waist, and I went back to bed feeling that it was something I shouldn't have seen.

Aki-Ko means autumn child, and was the name of my other grandmother. I once asked Pappa if she had been born in the fall. He didn't know. Birthday celebrations were a Western custom that hadn't arrived when he was a child. People often named their children names for no particular reason other than the sound of them, Pappa said. Natsu-Ko and Haru-Ko and Yuki-Ko were also popular pretty names evoking seasons. Pappa's name was Otto.

Aki-Ko wore her hair in a bun, like White-Haired Ba-Chan, but hers was spiky and fought to be released from its harsh metal pins. The bun was black and remained so, even as she aged, so I called her Black-Haired Ba-Chan. The bad grandmother.

It was late June and the water between the mainland and the island was brown and murky and calm. The ferry was crowded with tourists, eager to see the island's gold mines. My mother told me that convicts and orphans were once sent from the mainland to the island to work, and most times die, in the labyrinthian mines.

My aunt had reserved a private compartment for us on the ferry's third floor, but my mother spent most of the time outside in the damp wind, drinking tea. I sat next to her on a bench by the ferry's bow. She was composed, her gloved hands clasped around an empty paper tea cup in her lap, her legs pressed together tightly with one foot tucked behind the other.

I took my cues from my mother. If her face remained unlined and smooth, I would be quiet and happy. If a look of alarm crossed her face, a flicker of fear would reverberate through me. Today my mother appeared calm and reserved, so I took on her manner.

"What's it going to be like?" I asked. The wind whipped sharply around us. My chapped lips stung and tasted of salt when I licked them.

My mother turned to me. "You mean without White-Haired Ba-Chan?"

"No, at that place. The Yaki-Ba."

My mother picked up her paper tea cup and examined it.

"Many of your relatives will be there. Don't worry. It'll be fine."

I had never heard of the Yaki-Ba until White-Haired Ba-Chan died. It is the Japanese word for crematorium, but I could only think of it literally as the "burn place."

"Is Black-Haired Ba-Chan going to be at the Yaki-Ba?" I asked.

My mother nodded. She crumpled the tea cup in her hand and relaxed her grip, finger by finger, until the wind snapped the cup out and over the ferry's edge.

As the ferry approached the harbor, my mother pointed out the northern side of the island, all hard grassy hills and rocks. The southern side was covered with wet green trees and dotted with tiny wooden houses.

"No one lives in the north," my mother said.

"Pappa told me that he saw someone there once," I said. "An old man living in a cave."

My mother clucked her tongue and looked at me with a tired smile. "You mustn't believe his stories. He got that talent from his mother."

White-Haired Ba-Chan had lived on the southern tip of the island, in a large house with a carp pond and a vegetable garden in the backyard. My mother was born and reared there with my aunt and Uncle Ken, who both still lived there.

Black-Haired Ba-Chan lived farther to the north in a ramshackle house, partly hidden from the street by overgrown blackberry bushes and shrubs. The house was so small that she and Pappa had to share a room when he was growing up.

■ ■ ■

Later, at my aunt's house, my mother asked: "Is everything arranged?" She sipped tea with one flat palm supporting the bottom of the cup, and the other hand lightly wrapped around the center. My aunt nodded.

"Yes. Ken is already there. We should leave in a few hours."

I pretended to drink the tea, but it was bitter and raw, like grass. I could drink tea if cakes were served, which tasted even sweeter against the bitterness.

We sat on flat silk cushions in the sitting room, which had a high beamed ceiling and a floor covered with fragrant, new straw mats. My mother poured another cup of tea for my aunt.

"The house looks wonderful," my mother told her.

All the straw mats in the house had been replaced. They were always changed every summer, but usually not until August.

While my mother and aunt talked, I roamed around the house. Next to the sitting room was the great room, with wide windows overlooking the carp pond, where my mother's piano stood idle. I pressed down on a key softly. B flat, I thought, although I wasn't positive. Both White-Haired Ba-Chan and my mother played piano with skill.

Through the windows, I could see a large patch of uneven grass and weeds. Last summer, there had been eggplant, both white and purple, tomatoes and baby cucumbers, as well as impatiens and goldenboy. There were still plenty of fleshy carp, swimming in circles at the bottom of the pond, waiting to be fed.

I walked down a narrow hallway that led to the back of the house, and to White-Haired Ba-Chan's room.

The mirror atop the low table was gone, as was her large

comb. Her bedding, which she'd kept in a high pile in the closet, had been removed, and the closet was freshly painted white. A paper window, fully opened, let in a harsh column of sunlight through which floated particles of dust.

My aunt said White-Haired Ba-Chan had turned yellow right before she died. Jaundice, she said, often comes with cancer. I hoped that when the wooden coffin carrying White-Haired Ba-Chan was brought in to the Yaki-Ba, the lid would be opened, just for a moment, so I could see. But the coffin remained closed.

My uncles placed the coffin on a large iron tray and slid the tray deep into the oven and closed the door. About thirty relatives and friends, dressed in dark-colored clothes, watched in silence. My mother's eyes were downcast but dry.

The door of the oven was slightly rounded at top, with a small square window. Metal reinforcement bars ran the length of the door. Flames gradually appeared behind the window, first flickering gently, then raging. I sat close by the door so I could watch the orange flames. We waited a long time.

"My family never used gas," said Black-Haired Ba-Chan. She sat next to me, smoking.

"And it was done outdoors in the old days, close to the cemetery. The body was wrapped in a white kimono and then placed on a pile of wood. That's what we did with your pappa's father."

Black-Haired Ba-Chan inhaled deeply, and the cigarette burned down to her fingertips. She crushed the stub in an ashtray and lit a fresh cigarette.

I never knew my grandfather. He died of tuberculosis

long before I was born, but I imagined a handsome man who resembled Pappa. I pictured him lying on his back burning, skin blistering, smoke billowing around him.

The air in the room had grown stale, and I found it hard to breathe.

"Look, the flames have gone out," Black-Haired Ba-Chan said. She tugged at my sleeve and pointed with a cigarette to the oven.

The window was dark. I was relieved, hoping now that we could leave the Yaki-Ba, go outside into the fresh air, and return to my aunt's house.

"It's over?" I asked. Black-Haired Ba-Chan shook her head, loosening a hairpin, which dangled above her right ear.

"No, no. They have to let everything cool down now," she said.

But the room grew warmer and warmer. I wondered if the smell in the room was old incense, or White-Haired Ba-Chan's remains, or a combination of both.

There was nothing to look at on the walls, no paintings or drawings, not even a clock. My mother was speaking quietly to Uncle Ken at the other side of the room, never venturing in my direction. She had always disliked Black-Haired Ba-Chan, and since divorcing Pappa, she no longer spoke to her. Black-Haired Ba-Chan had come to the Yaki-Ba not to pay respects, but to see me, and she clung to my side. Pappa said I should spend time with her, because she was his mother and her blood ran in my veins. With White-Haired Ba-Chan gone, she was my only grandmother.

I had sided with my mother early on. White-Haired Ba-Chan had smelled like grandmothers should, sometimes of mothballs, or of eucalyptus cream or of nothing. Black-Haired Ba-Chan's perfume and stale cigarette smoke followed her whenever she came to visit. She burned holes in our blankets when she fell asleep smoking. She would let strange dogs into our house.

The Buddhist priest adjusted his collar. He was dressed in a heavy embroidered robe over a white kimono, and in his right hand was a small bronze bowl, which he hit with a wooden mallet. It gave off a deep, bell-like sound.

Black-Haired Ba-Chan had been dozing, but now snapped her head to attention, reaching instinctively for her pack of cigarettes. I looked across the room at my mother. Our eyes met for a moment, and she raised her eyebrows before getting up with my aunt and Uncle Ken.

Fresh sticks of incense burned in the corners of the room, filling the air with a sharp, slightly sweet odor. The priest began chanting in a monotonous drone that came from deep in his chest, singing words that ran one into the other, barely pausing for breath. He hit the bowl three times in succession.

The oven door opened. My uncles put on thick hand mittens and pulled out the large iron tray. My mother, my aunt, and Uncle Ken stood still, side by side next to the tray, until the priest began chanting again.

Using a pair of long, silver chopsticks, my mother gently picked up a large bone from the tray. It was the bone at the lower neck where the back begins. She looked perfectly calm, as if this were something she had rehearsed many times before. She placed the bone in a ceramic urn, then handed the urn and the chopsticks to my aunt.

The bones were burnt white. My aunt's hand shook as

she tried to grasp part of a rib, and she dropped it before reaching the urn. The bone landed back on the tray with a soft thud, in a puff of ash.

Black-Haired Ba-Chan sniffed and my aunt brought a hand quickly to her mouth in dismay. I took light, shallow breaths, afraid of inhaling particles of White-Haired Ba-Chan.

Uncle Ken selected a third bone with the chopsticks, deposited it in the urn, and passed along the chopsticks and the urn to the priest. The priest finished collecting the rest of the bones, and when he began sweeping up the ashes with a thick brush, we left.

It wasn't until evening that my aunt led me to White-Haired Ba-Chan's room. She opened one of the closets and from a high shelf, which I could not reach, pulled down a lacquered box.

"This is for you," my aunt said.

She handed me the box, then padded down the hallway to the kitchen to finish preparing dinner. The paper window in White-Haired Ba-Chan's room was open, and I could hear the voices of my mother and Uncle Ken on the back porch.

I lifted the lid slowly. White-Haired Ba-Chan rarely gave me presents.

Inside, the box was lined with pale pink silk. On the silk, coiled in the shape of a bird's nest, was my grandmother's hair. The hair was slightly yellow against the silk, the same shade as that morning when I saw her in front of her mirror.

I drew the box closer. There was no scent, except for the smell of smoke on the sleeves of my dress.

My Two Grandmothers

❧

By Arlynn S. Geers

I don't remember Grandmother Anna, my father's mother, very well because when I was about four years old the family had some sort of disagreement and did not keep in touch for many years. I was in my twenties when she passed on, and I do remember going to her funeral.

I'm sure she was a good person. My mother had two babies sixteen months apart, and Mother told me how Grandmother Anna would come to our home every Thursday to take care of my brother and me to give Mother some free time.

We had a high wooden gate in our backyard. My brother was just about three and he was always running out of the yard. Grandmother put a hook high upon the wooden gate but he would still get out. One day she watched him and noticed that he took a clothes pole and put it under the latch. The gate opened and he ran out. My grandmother cried out, "Come back here, you little Bummy." To this day I still call my six-foot-tall brother "Bummy."

My grandfather, whom I never knew, worked for the United Railway Company in St. Louis. The company ran the streetcars in St. Louis. Grandfather was an inventor and I remember hearing he invented the machinery that ripped up the tracks and that many other ideas the company used were his. The company would purchase large tracts of land out a distance from the city. Granddad and his crew would survey the land and then build large amusement parks there. The company would then put down tracks and the streetcars would take large crowds to these parks. They built Meramec Highlands, Forest Park Highlands, and Creve Coeur Lake Park. The streetcars were open on the sides and you could just step onto them. You could take a picnic lunch and stay at the park all day and evening. There was always a large dance floor, racer dips, and other amusements.

When Granddad surveyed these areas, my dad would go along and help. Grandmother would have to cook for all the men working on these jobs. Years later I saw the huge iron pot she cooked in. I heard she was a wonderful cook. I suppose my brother, Bob, got this talent from her. He had a restaurant in Hawthorne, California, for many years.

Caroline was my mother's mother. Caroline and her brother came to America from Melle, Germany, when she was about eighteen years old. They arrived in America on July 4, 1875.

Caroline's brother left her in St. Louis with a friend of his and he headed west to find his fortune. The lady with whom Caroline stayed ran a boardinghouse, and the farmers from Illinois brought their produce to the markets in St. Louis, then went to this boardinghouse for their lunch. On one very busy day the lady asked Caroline to help wait on the tables. My granddad was there eating his lunch and met Caroline. Two weeks later they were married. He gave her a beautiful gold pin and earrings to match. He took her to Illinois, where he had a farm. He was also studying to become a Lutheran minister. I might mention here that she spoke no English and Granddad spoke no German.

Caroline was not a farmwoman and she did not like the farm. One year they had a terrible flood and they lost everything. At that time they moved to Baden in St. Louis. Granddad got a job at the St. Louis Car Company. They manufactured streetcars for all over the country. My grand-dad, an uncle, my father, and my husband all worked at one time or another at the St. Louis Car Company.

Caroline and Granddad had eight children, four of whom lived. My mother was the youngest of the eight.

Caroline was only about five feet tall and never weighed over one hundred pounds. She was very prim and proper. I heard she was one of the best dancers in her village in Germany and that she spoke excellent High German.

From the time I was little, she seemed elderly and old-fashioned to me. She wore long skirts and blouses with high collars and long sleeves. In the winter she wore a little fur cape and a small bonnet that tied under her chin. Every-thing had to be done on the same day each week: wash clothes on Monday; iron on Tuesday; and the kitchen floor was always scrubbed on Sunday. She would take up the newspapers from the previous week, wash the floor, and put down fresh newspaper. I still cannot understand this. The parlor was never opened except for funerals or a wedding. After Granddad died, the oldest son came home to live with her. His wife had died in childbirth and Grandmother Caroline reared the baby boy. After this baby was grown and married, Grandmother came to live with my husband and me at our home. She never talked much, although she could now speak English and she read the newspapers every day. She never wore any makeup, and when she saw me put some on, she never said anything. She just looked at me and shook her head.

She passed away when she was eighty-six. Now when I look back I wish I had had more conversations with her and asked her about her early life. I also wish I had learned to speak German . . . but at that time I did not think I would ever have any use for it.

My Emotional Grandmother

By Doris Moore

Both of my grandmothers had gone to the great beyond before they played any part in my life. I have just turned ninety-seven and my sister is only a bit younger. Our biological grandmothers would be very, very old. I can, however, think of one of my mother's friends, a Mrs. Pegram, whom we called Didam, who lived in an apartment in Washington. She was my emotional grandmother. Didam entered our lives at a very early date, for I can never remember a time when she was not there ready to help my mother take care of her three young children. The apartment house where she lived, the Prince Carl, was a very handsome big building, the first big apartment house built in Washington, and I think it may still be in use. These are memories of a very early time in my life, so I cannot vouch for everything. You will just have to take my word.

Didam would invite me to spend a weekend with her at the Prince Carl. I would go to town on Saturday morning with my father when he went to work on the train, and Didam would meet me at the station in Washington. From that time until Monday evening Didam and I would sightsee and shop in the big merchandise stores and I would learn about all the city sights and sounds that were so foreign to a country girl. However, by Monday I'd be homesick, and by the time my father picked me up Monday evening to go back to Falls Church and my family, it took very little persuasion for me to leave.

Didam had a very handsome grown daughter, Nan, who lived with her and who worked for one of the senators at the Capitol. At various times Didam would take me to the Capitol to find out about life there and eventually to receive an appointment with Senator Shouse, who was a senator from Kansas at that time. This was when the First World War started and it was a very exciting time. I remember that the stairway to the Capitol tower had been closed to visitors for the period of the war, but the officer in charge of the building got a special pass for me to go up in it. I got up all right and I could see all over Washington, but when I tried to make the trip down, my country upbringing must have taken over and they had to send one of the guards to help me.

Also, when I was invited at Christmastime to go to the Center Market in Washington, a tremendous market even in those days, it was nothing short of a miracle to me after our little country store with its horse-drawn wagon, and I can still remember those oranges and other fruits and nuts. Korn also had a rather primitive soda fountain in their store, where Didam took me every time for a soda. One day when we visited the fountain I sat next to a very dressed-up lady. In those days ladies wore thin white linen skirts. This particular day was the first time I had ever had a chocolate soda in a glass with a straw, and being unfamiliar with the procedure, I blew in the straw. You can imagine what happened to the lady's white blouse and skirt.

When the spring came Didam would spend quite a lot of time with us in Falls Church. She loved flowers and would buy many different kinds of seeds. In those days we planted petunias, nasturtiums, lady slippers, and all the others there was room for, and in a week or two our yard would be a picture.

Spring on the Potomac River was shad season, just like it is fried catfish season down here. Didam would stop at the Center Market on her way to Falls Church and buy a shad. They were usually about four or five pounds and were cooked in our big turkey roaster for most of Saturday afternoon. What a wonderful dinner we would have.

I cannot remember exactly how long Didam remained as my emotional grandmother, but I am sure it was long enough to give me the ability to cope with all those new and interesting people and experiences I was to encounter during my working years.

A Union of Confederates

⌀∕⌀

By *Anna W. Kenney*

I had two grandmothers who grew up on opposite sides of the Mason-Dixon line, but both of my grandfathers were Confederate soldiers.

My Virginia grandmother was born in 1864 and was not quite eighteen years old when her sweetheart and neighbor was wounded at the Battle of Spotsylvania Courthouse in the Wilderness Campaign. This was the same day and battle in which Stonewall Jackson was killed. Grandfather was a sergeant in Lee's cavalry and not quite twenty years old. His wound was thought to be fatal, as the bullet had entered his neck. He was brought home to die. (I have a copy of the note my grandmother's father wrote to the clerk giving her permission to be married because it would otherwise not be proper for her to go to his home to help take care of him.) However, Grandfather lived. The bullet worked its way neatly around all vital organs and came out of his lower back. A great-grandson is the proud owner of that bullet. Grandfather lived until 1902; he died sixteen weeks before my birth.

My grandmother continued to live in the big old house across the street from us with her oldest daughter, who was unmarried, and Elvira, a slave girl who had been given to her the day Grandmother was born. I remember her as the traditional grandmother, wrapping up stumped toes and giving us candy and cookies. Times were hard in the South after the war, and a young couple had to work very hard to bring up and educate their children. She had done that by the time I knew her. When her arthritis and diabetes put her in bed, she traded the big old house with her youngest son and moved down the street near my other grandmother. She died when I was eight years old.

My northern grandmother came to Page County, Virginia, from the Emma Willard School in Troy, New York, as a governess in the home of Mr. and Mrs. Ruben Bell. She soon met and fell in love with Mrs. Bell's young brother. By the time he went into the war, they had two little girls. Grandfather was in an artillery company and his eardrums were damaged by the constant blast of the cannons. He came home in bad shape. I don't remember all the details, but they were living in Lynchburg, where he was in business with his brother when my mother was married and moved to Chatham. After Grandfather's death, Grandmother bought a house in Chatham and moved there with her two sisters and her youngest daughter. This was the year I was two years old.

By the time I was five, one of Grandmother's older sisters had died and her youngest daughter had married. So now I just had Grandmother and her sister, whom we called Aunt Mie (her name was Almira), who was like a third grandmother.

Aunt Mie had gone from the Emma Willard School in Troy to teach in Cincinnati, Ohio, where she taught for

forty-one years. She was seventy-four years old and Grandmother was seventy. She had taught William Howard Taft
and his brother, Robert, who sent her birthday and
Christmas cards for the rest of her life.

That year that I was five, she had a little school for
relatives and neighbor children in the back room upstairs.
This was my school. My brother had already been going to
Miss Lucy Ballard's school on the other side of town. My
sister, who was fifteen months younger than me, was still
just four and so she didn't go to school yet.

Aunt Mie had things we had never seen. A big, beautiful
abacus with bright-colored beads was used to teach us to
add, subtract, and multiply. She had books with stories we
hadn't heard and poems to memorize. All the stories had a
moral or taught us the value of good manners. We learned
about Indians by memorizing "Hiawatha." We learned
about the Arcadians from the poem "Evangeline." We
memorized beautiful passages from the Bible and lovely old
hymns. It was an introduction to the world.

Grandmother's house continued to be both a refuge and
an inspiration. To come in from the cold into the cozy
dining room with its open-faced Franklin stove and bub-
bling copper teakettle and old Terry clock ticking away on
the mantel was sheer joy. I would go immediately to the
sideboard for the "Flinch" cards, kept in the left-hand
drawer, and begin to deal the hands. There were Grandmother, Aunt Mie, and Mrs. Dagger, a neighbor, and others
who were not "regulars." We would settle down for a hand
or two while the bread or cake baked. Then Grandmother
would let me help serve the tea (cumbrie tea, hot water, and
milk for us; real tea for them). Nothing since then has tasted
so good.

Grandmother was tiny, never more than ninety pounds

and a little less than five feet tall. She played the old flat-topped rosewood piano and sang the Civil War songs in her sweet plaintive voice. Some days we found Grandmother and Aunt Mie reading aloud to each other. They would catch us up on the story and we would listen to the rest.

They lived on in their house until one summer when my aunt in Lynchburg came for a visit and saw Grandmother coming downstairs with a lighted kerosene lamp in one hand and an armful of bed linen in the other. My aunt did not comment on that, but the next morning when she came down to help with breakfast, she saw her mother pour kerosene into the wood stove and strike a match to it. The flame rose three feet in the air. With that she issued an ultimatum: Grandmother and Aunt Mie would have to either go back to live with her in Lynchburg or move in with us.

To our joy, they chose us. Aunt Mie helped us with our homework and we read aloud to her. Grandmother taught us to sew and knit and helped with our piano practice. They had been brought up as Quaker Abolitionists, and when fate brought them to southern Virginia, they befriended and helped the colored people in every way they could, so finding somebody to help care for them was no problem.

Grandmother died the fall I went to college. She was eighty-three.

Aunt Mie lived on for three more years. One day she came down to breakfast and said that she had not slept well and thought she would go back upstairs and lie down for a little while. When Mother went up a little later, she was gone. She was ninety-one. That was 1923. I had had them for twenty-one years and would never forget them.

My Russian Grandmother

By *Rosel Schewel*

My grandmother (my mother's mother) lived until after I was married. I grew up in the town where she lived, and I know that I went with my mother to visit her every Saturday, but for some reason I remember very little about her. I can describe exactly how she looked, though. She was a small woman, with a very round, pretty face that was deeply lined. Her hair was not totally gray, and she wore it in a very plain style, tied in a bun in the back. I remember her mostly wearing dark dresses covered by an apron.

My grandmother came to this country from Riga, Latvia, as a young adult and was married shortly after arriving. In my dining room, I have the samovar that was sent to her from Russian relatives as a wedding present. If she ever used it, she did so long before I can remember. I always saw her drinking tea at her round oak dining room table, pouring from a Chinese teapot.

Maybe I don't remember conversations, trips, or playtime with my grandmother because she spoke very little English. She spoke Yiddish, which is a combination of Hebrew and German and was (and still is) the conversational, colloquial language of Jews all over the world. My parents wanted me to become totally assimilated into the American scene and so did not encourage me to learn Yiddish. They wanted me to answer my grandmother in English, even if she asked me a question in Yiddish. Unfortunately, I never learned Yiddish except for a few common expressions. Several times while traveling in Russia and Europe I wished I had known Yiddish because it would have been a way to communicate with Jews from all over the world.

In retrospect, I think my parents wanted my grandmother to learn from me, rather than me learn from her. I don't remember her ever telling me stories of the "old country," what the circumstances surrounding her leaving were, what her life had been like, etc. I think this was characteristic of Jewish families at that time who were eager to forget their difficult experiences and to assimilate into the American scene as quickly as possible.

There is one regular ritual of my grandmother's that I do remember participating in with her, and which has probably been an important influence on my life. Nailed to the cabinet doors under my grandmother's sink were four or five "pushkies"—little metal boxes with slits in the top to receive money—with the name of a particular charity written on the front of each box. Each Saturday when my mother and I went to visit my grandmother, before we left her house, she would put some coins in each of the pushkies and we would follow along after her and do the same. I remember thinking it was a lot of fun and somehow got the feeling from her that by doing this we were helping others. About once a month, a person working for a particular one of these charitable groups would stop by her house and empty that particular pushky. The person collecting would go from house to house in that neighborhood and collect from each person's little metal box marked with that charity's name.

As I reflect on it, I don't feel that my grandmother thought that she was intentionally teaching me to be helpful and charitable. I think she was just serious about trying to raise a little money for poor immigrant Jews, and she wanted money from as many family members as possible. Perhaps this was the beginning of the many fund drives we have today . . . perhaps it is where I got my sense of the importance of supporting good and needy causes. Since I remember that practice so well, and not many others, it clearly left a lasting impression.

I also remember my grandmother's Passover Seders. All of the women in the family gathered at my grandmother's rather small home the day or two before Seder night to help prepare for this family gathering. A long table was constructed in her dining room by putting wood boards over wooden horses, which were stored in her basement for this yearly purpose. The women in the family cooked for days in advance and my cousins, aunts, and uncles squeezed into her dining room to read the traditional Seder service and enjoy the Passover dinner. All that I remember of those evenings was, as a small child, laughing and talking and crawling under the long table . . . and squirting the seltzer bottles. Seltzer was a soda water that came in bottles with pressure levers that one pushed to squirt the seltzer in the glass with wine to make a delicious drink traditionally enjoyed during Passover. Although I have warm memories of those Seder nights, I remember no other details. I continue those big family Seders in my own home with lots of young grandchildren making noise and crawling around under the long table, just as my grandmother did two generations earlier.

Grandmother

By Ellison Smythe

My maternal grandmother was Mrs. James (Amey) Allan, late of Rutledge Avenue in Charleston, South Carolina. Grandma Allan came to Charleston from London in the 1830s or '40s. I wasn't around at the time, so the exact date of her arrival escapes me. However, Mrs. James (Amey Hobcraft) Allan was never backward about letting you know in no uncertain terms that she was a Br-r-r-ritish subject during the reign of good Queen Victoria, and was proud of the fact that the sun never set on the Empire's flag! In fact, she flew the British Union Jack from the second-story porch of their four-story "sidewise,"—a one-room-wide house that was designed to catch a sea breeze through each room, and that had porches on each floor the full length of the house. Her husband, James Allan, came from Wick, in North Scotland, with his father at age seven. He served in the Confederate forces during the Civil War, first on a blockade-runner and then as a foot soldier.

During the war, when Sherman's stragglers were looting anything of value they could, a drunk Yankee soldier started up the steps of Grandma's home. Grandma stood at the top and said, "You cannot come in. I am a Br-r-r-ritish subject! See that flag!" The soldier cursed her and started to push past her. She gave him a sudden shove. He lost his balance and tumbled down the long flight of steps to the street. Staggering to his feet, he cursed and shook his fist and left.

Although both Grandma and Grandpa were opposed to slavery, it was almost impossible in Charleston in that day to get the domestic help they needed without buying a slave family: the man to serve as coachman and look after the horse and yard; his wife to cook in the kitchen house in back of the main house; one of the family to work as a maid; and a girl to handle odd chores.

After Appomattox, James Allan made his way back to Charleston and arrived dirty, bearded, tired. When he started up the steps at his house, from which the Union Jack was still flying, he was accosted by Grandma with the command: "You cannot come in here! I'm a Br-r-r-ritish subject." He responded: "Why, Amey! Don't you recognize me? I'm your husband, Jamey."

Shortly before his return home, Grandma thought she heard someone in the back lot trying to steal the horse. She grabbed a pistol off the table and went out in the dark to scare off any intruder but could find no one. On her return to the house, her oldest son said, "What would you have done if there had been someone out there? That old gun is not loaded." She replied fiercely, "Then I would have thrown it at him."

My personal recollections of Grandma were of her later years. Her husband had built up a thriving jewelry business and, being Scottish, he invested wisely and they prospered. They also "thrived" family-wise, having eight or ten children. My grandmother used to sit in her chair in the living room with a circle of us children listening to her old English songs and stories. One of our favorites was about the King of the Cannibal Islands. The climax would come when the Cannibal King reached for a victim to devour and Grandma would make a grab at the nearest child. We would scatter and scream and it all ended in laughter and the plea "Do it again, Grandma."

Grandma was very generous with her considerable wealth. She helped financially support a couple of homes for war widows and older women, and she also spent time visiting with them. I remember all too vividly when I was allowed to ride in the seat with Dan, the coachman, on one of her visits. I was perched on the driver's seat when Dan opened the big yard gate, and when the horse started through the gate onto the street, I picked up the reins. The horse must have thought that meant that Dan was in the driver's seat, so it increased its speed down the street. I pulled on the reins and the harder I pulled the faster it went. Dan was running behind trying to catch us. He yelled to some men down the street to stop the runaway with the small kid pulling on the reins. Fortunately, one of the men caught the horse's bridle. Dan had to drive on around the block and stopped at the door to pick up Grandma, who gave us a stiff lecture and told me never to touch the horse's reins again.

The old lady lived to be over ninety and gave up her British citizenship only when she was told by the command officer of the Union army of Occupation in Charleston that he could not give her and her property protection unless she became an American citizen. However, no one could ever take away her Br-r-r-ritish way of speaking.

A Grandmotherless Child

By Kathleen Carroll Bailey Angle

At fifty, I am still a grandmotherless child and I am afraid. I am terrified of meeting Grandmother Bailey. She died when I was four years old and there are no memories, only pictures; pictures of a very stern woman looking very mean, always dressed in black and always standing.

Last summer I was forced to meet Grandmother. There was no choice once the book, *The Report of the Secretary of Agriculture 1890,* was placed in my hands by my ninety-year-old aunt Kathleen.

Holding this faded worn brown book protected by a heavy clear plastic bag, I realized that I must come to terms with my South Carolina tears. Why is it that every time I leave South Carolina for home, for Virginia, I begin to cry? Why am I so apprehensive about opening this book? I tell myself, Be brave, don't be shy, don't be afraid of meeting Janie Brown Bailey. She is your grandmother.

For at fifty a grandmotherless child lives in me, still craves that special feeling that only a grandmother can give. I long to be a granddaughter and feel that bond, that unconditional love flowing, building the inner belief that lasts a lifetime that convinces the granddaughter, yes, indeed, she is someone special.

As I stood at the kitchen table and slowly opened the pages of her book, tattered and faded newspaper clippings fell crumbling into my fingers—no way for me to save all of the pieces of heritage slipping into slivers of dust. Pick the paper up slowly, Kathleen, hold it gently, gently touch the brown pieces of newsprint still strong enough to stand the pressure of shaking, frightened, yet curious fingers. Filter, filter the words staring up through one hundred years and discover the stern grandmother of faded photographs on black pages. Read the tiny columns of print until a grandmother is born, until she becomes flesh and bone, heart and soul, a real memory.

It's so strange to hold this book, her book with such an unusual title, *The Report of the Secretary of Agriculture 1890,* and find its contents so diverse, so changed by Grandmother's hands, by Grandmother's scissors.

I am so frightened. Do I want to touch the hands that held this thick faded brown book? To feel the fingers that so carefully placed clippings in its pages, some sewn on the page with tiny pieces of pink thread, others near the end of the book glued on the page? Do I want to see the face, gaze into the eyes, and sense the person who looked upon these faded fragile pieces of newsprint? Do I want to know the lady who saved these poetic words? Do I want to talk with her, to hear her voice reading to me? Do I really want to meet you, Grandmother?

The decaying pieces of newspaper articles called me. Tattered pieces of poetry, death notices, World War I stories, lists of war dead, words seventy-five to one hundred years old became tangled inside me and blended with the mental picture of a petite lady I never knew except in photographs. So many questions.

Did my father's name, hence my middle name, Carroll, come from the "History of the Liberty Bell" article? The spelling is unusual and not often used as a boy's name. Was he named after Charles Carroll of Carrollton, Maryland, the last surviving signer of the Declaration of Independence?

Grandmother, calm my fears. Read the poems to me, Grandmother; tell me of your dreams. Am I like you? Did my love for poetry, for literature, come from you? Which pieces were your favorites? Are they the ones you sewed in the book? Or did you manage to get some glue to paste in your favorites on top of the agriculture pages that told of animals and crops?

What of the local news articles, wedding announcements, and death notices? Were the Tubervilles and Harts your friends or relatives, cousins whose names are not accessible to me? What was the significance of the list of soldiers, the war dead?

Who was Thomas Cottingham? The news article stated, ". . . with General Pershing's troops, fell in action." What about Captain W. T. Shaw, who soon after his marriage to Miss Blanche Stanton sailed for France and was "killed in battle"? Did the war wrench your insides?

Oh, Grandmother, I am still scared, yet I could spend days reading and trying to enter your faraway world, to somehow merge your world with mine, to know you and your days of existence on this earth. If only I could have known you as a young girl, a wife, a mother, a friend, a South Carolinian, a Southerner, and an American. I cannot imagine what it must have been like to marry at thirteen and live in the sandy tobacco soil of Latta, South Carolina. Yet there is something about that flat land of sand spurs that calls me, talks to me.

Every summer when I return to the Palmetto State, I sense the land, I feel its energy, and I seem to know and yet know not what I know of the land's voice. Leaving Virginia, I travel the back roads of North and South Carolina. I drive through Whiteville, Fair Bluff, Lake View, Mullens, Marion, and eventually cross the Pee Dee River near Florence. The land talks to me, and like the gray moss-draped elms and lazy swamps, I feel calm. I belong to this land, this place where the blacktop roads slice through the tobacco and cotton fields, passing the weatherworn tobacco sheds and faded houses. Northeast South Carolina's fields, swamps, and country roads have a hold on me.

The tall ladder-back rocking chair on the front porch greets me with Southern hospitality. I feel welcome. Now, Grandmother, perhaps as I read the poems and articles in your book, I come closer to the answer.

Perhaps this hostage, your granddaughter, will finally know why the land of sweet tea and grits speaks to me and holds me in its mystical spell—a spell I have never been able to share with anyone, it seems so eerie. I couldn't even explain South Carolina's hold on me to my younger sister. South Carolina means nothing to her. It is just a place where some of our relatives happen to live.

Ah, it's you, isn't it, Grandmother? It's the romantic you who calls me and draws me to this land. I hold your book in my hands, I see the poems, I can feel you looking over my shoulder, reading these words on friendship, emphasizing those poetic words on self-worth, reciting the poems about motherhood.

As the scissors carefully trim the articles, I imagine you agonizing over the dying Confederate soldier's poem to his mother, interpreting President Wilson's comments, laughing at the humorous poem on the Latta baseball team, with its record of 10–0, and at the same time knowing of the winners' excitement through your eldest son, Harvey. I visualize a young girl in love with the fall and at the same time searching for knowledge as she clips an article explaining "fall colors." October is my favorite time of year.

I am overwhelmed by this homemade scrapbook and the grandmother emerging from its pages. It is so strange to see the pencil marks, your marks in a scribble much like mine, marking your birth date, your wedding date, and the birth dates of my four uncles and Aunt Kathleen, and finally my father's date written on a separate page, the last one, the youngest of your children.

And suddenly I see a name I do not recognize, a baby who died—is that why you saved some of those bizarre articles on the death of children, which seemed so out of place among the poems?

Oh, Grandmother, hold my hand, it is still so hard to see you through the low-lying fog of eighty, ninety, one hundred years ago, through the mossy black-water swamps of South Carolina. It is so hard not to be frightened. I look to the poetry again to find words that will temper the image created by family photo albums. You look so harsh with round wire-rimmed glasses hiding your eyes. What color were they? You look so formidable, so cold with straight black hair pulled tight against your head, ending in a thick bun. You look like someone a child would fear, yet the words you saved contradict the photographer's image that has lived in my mind for so long. The words, the poems, are the key.

Tears always overwhelm me when I leave South Carolina, when I cross the Pee Dee River. The tears stream down my cheeks, and driving always becomes so difficult as the tears turn into sobs. I always want to turn back and I always wonder why. Why am I sobbing like this? I don't think about it and it happens every time.

It's you I've been searching for all these years, Grandmother, it is you who haunts this tearful grandmotherless child. It's you I am discovering in the pages of agriculture among the tattered brown clippings. Hello, Grandmother. Was pink your favorite color?

PART THREE

"Over the river and through the woods
To Grandmother's house we go . . ."
—LYDIA MARIA CHILD

Grandmother

By Kyoko Mori

On the blue aerogramme,
her Japanese brushstrokes are mayflies
fluttering away from me.
She's taken flowers to Grandpa's grave—
peonies this month.
With each letter, her brushstrokes grow
more tenuous, threatening
to evaporate altogether.
Still, she stands on the dirt road
between the house and the family cemetery,
her arms around the peonies
two wisps of smoke—
while mayflies swirl
into blue air merging
dotted shadows with hers.

I Have a Memory Trace

By *Mary King*

My great-great-great-grandfather Wright Johnson pulled on his sturdiest boots. The soles had been repaired again and again, and, in preparation for this trip, they had again been resoled. He was wearing heavy homespun wool pants, a homespun wool jacket with wide lapels, a white shirt with billowing sleeves, and a sash tied loosely at the neck. His deerskin jacket was made from a buck he had shot himself, as were his gloves. He pulled low on his forehead a raccoon hat that would shield him from the rain. As he sat on the edge of his handmade wooden bed, he placed the last few items, including his Bible, in his satchel of wild boar skin.

It was the winter of 1836. He stepped out of his log house built from hewn timbers in Surry County, North Carolina, near the state line just below Patrick County, Virginia. He was leaving behind his wife, Nancy Wilkes, who came from Wilkes County, North Carolina. Her light blond "flaxen hair" caught the light as she stood in the window to wave good-bye. He closed the hatched door, thinking, *It smells like snow*—in that peculiar vernacular of farmers and those who live close to the land and can sense when it's going to snow. Ahead of him lay a 275-mile walk to be ordained a deacon in the Methodist Church.

Wright Johnson had been preaching for many years as a licensed lay preacher, or "local preacher," to use the church term. His grandfather had been an officer of the Virginia militia who fell in Braddock's defeat in the French and Indian War in 1755. But now Wright Johnson wanted to be an officer in the army of the spirit—he was determined to become a full-fledged minister in the first of the two categories of ordination provided by the Methodist *Discipline* and would soon be able to administer the ordinances of baptism, marriage, and burial of the dead.

The records of the "class meeting" that he supervised some years later at the Mount Hermon Methodist Church in Surry County foreshadow my own interest in human rights and show an openness of spirit that was ahead of his time. Among those noted in the meticulously kept attendance records for 1849, with a cursive "P" for present and "A" for absent, are two black women members of his class, listed as "colored members." It was commonplace before the Emancipation Proclamation for slaves to attend church with their masters, sitting in a separate balcony, which can still be seen in some church buildings. But the class meeting was an altogether different phenomenon. At the heart of membership in the early Methodist Church was the idea of close personal fellowship obtainable only in a small group. Ministers—sometimes called circuit riders—traveling the frontier on horseback with twenty, thirty, or more preaching places could not know each member individually. Class meetings were an important supplement, with class leaders chosen to act as lay pastors. With usually no more than twelve members, class meetings gathered weekly for Bible study, individual witness, prayer, discipline, spiritual guidance, and problem solving. These were close personal sessions—not formal worship in the sanctuary—in which everyone knew everyone else intimately, and class or social distinctions were set aside as each member participated freely. The doctrine of free grace for all brought about an insistence on the worth of each person under God. Despite the emphasis on democracy and participation, during the years before the Civil War, black or slave members would have been restricted to sitting in balconies during regular worship. The fact that these two black women, "colored members," were regular members of my great-great-great-grandfather's intimate class meeting is surprising, at a time when the United States had admitted little more than half its eventual quota of states to the Union.

The circuit riders and their assistants—the class leaders and lay preachers—were involved in the total fabric of eighteenth- and nineteenth-century American society. They agitated for improved social conditions, they were booksellers, and through their camp meetings they helped lay the groundwork for democratic self-government. They also acted as physicians of sorts in emergencies.

Starting out on that overcast day in 1836, Wright Johnson walked from Surry County approximately seventy-five miles to Danville in Pittsylvania County, Virginia, breaking his journey by staying overnight with kinfolk along the way. When he reached Danville, he spent an extra day resting in the home of a friend. Carrying his boar-skin satchel, he set out the next morning to walk the additional two hundred miles to Norfolk. He walked and walked, staying one night with a cousin and another night with strangers who took him into their home, sensing his faith, his determination, and understanding his mission. Weeks later, both his boot soles and his body thinner, he reached the meeting of the

Virginia Annual Conference of the Methodist Episcopal Church at Norfolk. After due examination and the recommendation of his peers, he was ordained by Bishop Elijah Hedding as a deacon of the church on February 17, 1836. The Reverend Wright Johnson then left Norfolk and walked the 275 miles back again across southside Virginia, stopping in Danville, to return home to his ministry.

Exactly 127 years later, I arrived in Danville, a tobacco and textile city of forty-five thousand, on June 22, 1963, in a shimmying red truck. I was traveling with Sam Shirah, a white native of Alabama, and another child of a Methodist minister, who had once been a student of George Wallace, later the avowedly segregationist governor of Alabama. Wallace had been his Sunday-school teacher in the town of Clayton. Sam joined the SNCC (Student Nonviolent Coordinating Committee) staff in May 1963 and led a Freedom Walk of ten persons into Alabama, a protest that had continued the "walk" of Baltimore postman William L. Moore, a member of CORE (Congress of Racial Equality), who was murdered on an Alabama highway at Attalla carrying signs protesting racial discrimination. As a result, Sam had spent thirty-two days on death row in the Kilby corrections facility, where the Scottsboro Boys were incarcerated—the nine black youths who were charged with the rape of two white women on a freight train in 1931 and, despite medical testimony to the contrary, were sentenced to death until the decision was reversed by the Supreme Court in 1932. We left the Atlanta SNCC headquarters, driving to New York City with an old friend of mine, Alan Hogenauer, in order to pick up the red truck that had been donated to the movement. Jim Forman

thought the truck ought to be assigned to the Danville
project and told me, as he dispatched us, that SNCC
workers Ivanhoe Donaldson, Bob Zellner, Dorothy Miller,
and Avon Rollins were expecting us at the local office in
Danville.

At midnight on June 19, Sam and I climbed into the
donated red truck, leaving Manhattan through the Holland
Tunnel for an overnight drive to my parents' home in
Virginia. On June 21, possessing the high energy of youth
that draws little distinction between night and day, we
roared out of Spotsylvania County at nine-thirty P.M. and
arrived at the movement headquarters in Danville early the
next morning. As we entered the city—briefly the last
capital of the Confederacy—I peered at it sprawling on the
banks of the Dan River. The main industry in Danville, the
Dan River Mills, was considered by the local chamber of
commerce to be the largest "single-unit textile mill in the
world," and it was the Dan River Mills that ran the town.

I was looking for four churches of which my grandfather,
the Reverend William Luther King, had been the pastor in
the 1920s—the Stokesland, Olivet, Fairview, and Design
congregations of the "Danville Circuit" of the Methodist
Episcopal Church, South. In the back of my mind was my
great-great-great-grandfather's journey on foot through
Danville and the handmade deerskin gloves from the buck
he had shot.

I still have Wright Johnson's oatmeal-colored deerskin
gloves with their crude but sturdy dark-brown stitches. I
had often fingered those gloves as a child. When I began to
ponder myself in place and time, the deerskin gloves gave
me hints and clues to the question that started in childhood
and persisted into my late twenties: Who am I? They told
me that I came from people who lived in wilderness and

helped to open up the country. Because of what I knew about Wright Johnson's steps, the gloves revealed tenacity and resourcefulness. They also said that my family lacked earthly riches but could survive on the land. From what I knew about the man who shot the buck and made the gloves, they told of a family with dignity and integrity that derived from a deep religious faith.

We passed Stratford College. This junior college was a continuation of the former Randolph-Macon Institute, a private and of course racially segregated and exclusive "ladies' seminary" affiliated with the Methodist Church. By special permission, my father, then a boy of thirteen, was allowed to attend along with his sister without having to pay tuition. This must have been a blessing because my grandfather's salary was then not much more than one hundred dollars a month. My father had been one of only two boys to have had that special status on the all-girls campus, the other being the son of Mr. Charles Evans, the principal of Randolph-Macon Institute.

I remembered that I had been to Danville only twice before, once as a small child and later, at thirteen, on the way to a reunion of my father's family in Patrick County, Virginia. Because of my experiences the previous year traveling with the human-relations project, I figured that I had only a few hours in Danville to observe and get my bearings before I would be targeted by the police. I knew that once I visited the movement's headquarters, from then on I would be marked and under scrutiny. I searched the city, imagining my father's boyhood days, my grandparents' lives, and, before that, Wright Johnson's sojourn there.

Sam and I arrived at the High Street Baptist Church, where Dorothy Miller would brief us on what had happened so far. We arrived at eight A.M. on Saturday morning.

Less than an hour later, I heard the Danville police, upstairs, kicking in the main door to the sanctuary of the church to arrest three SNCC workers who had been indicted by the grand jury.

I had come to Danville to run SNCC's local communications operation. I would manage everything related to the information we gave the news media representatives who were based in Danville and act as the telephone link between our Danville office and SNCC headquarters in Atlanta, from where Julian Bond would back me up if I was having trouble breaking a story. Dorothy Miller had been responsible for this function but was leaving for Massachusetts to enlarge the Boston Friends of SNCC group, one of our northern support organizations.

The following Monday morning, June 24, I attended a hearing before Federal Judge Thomas Jefferson Michie of the U.S. District Court for the Western District of Virginia. In the federal courthouse in Danville, motions were filed by several attorneys to remove the cases of two local men, jailed by Judge Archibald M. Aiken, from the state courts to the federal system. I watched a beautiful young black woman with presence named Ruth Harvey Charity, a local attorney who was the first woman lawyer in the city, making the motions. She and a team of noteworthy outside attorneys—Len Holt, William Kunstler, Arthur Kinoy, Professor Chet Antieu, Shellie F. Bowers (later a District of Columbia Superior Court judge), and Phil Hirschkopf, then a law student—were, along with five other local lawyers, to make a series of legal pirouettes that summer in Danville. The noted black attorney Leo Branton, brother of lawyer Wiley A. Branton, also came to Danville for a period from Los Angeles. Bill Kunstler treated me like a daughter and Ruth Harvey was warm and responsive to me, but it was Len Holt who would help me when the time came to escape across the river.

I had been in Danville for exactly two days. As I walked down the corridor to the courtroom of the federal courthouse, one of two tobacco-chewing Danville police lounging there called out loudly, "Mary King!" I was stunned. Even though I had tried to prepare myself mentally for being placed under close watch by the police in Danville, here was the evidence. I shuddered involuntarily. Forty-eight hours after my arrival, the police recognized me and knew my name.

Frustration had been brewing in the black community for some time. Inspired by the sit-ins that had started in 1960 not far away in Greensboro, North Carolina, the black leadership of Danville took action. For several months, there continued an intense legal skirmish concerning the main public library—the site of the final full cabinet meeting of the Confederacy—because blacks in Danville were not allowed to use this library. They were forced to use a pathetic branch typical of those to which blacks were relegated all over the region. Faced with a court order to desegregate, won by the NAACP, library officials closed the building from September through November 1960. It was then reopened on an integrated basis; however, all the chairs had been removed. For months afterward, admission to this previously free public library cost $2.50 for a one-year card.

One-third of Danville's population was black. In addition to their being disenfranchised, everything in the city was segregated. Streets in the black community were unpaved and badly lighted. Garbage was collected there less frequently than in the white community. Blacks were restricted to balconies in theaters. Restaurants, hotels, and motels bore WHITE ONLY signs. Restrooms at public facilities and gas stations were segregated. Physicians and dentists had two separate waiting rooms, one for whites and one for "colored." The train and bus stations had separate waiting rooms on either side of the station, similarly labeled. All the schools were segregated except for one state-financed vocational school for high school graduates that had admitted two black students the year before. By 1963, one of these had dropped out, leaving one sole black student in the entire area studying in an integrated institution.

Toward the end of May 1963, soon after television coverage flashed around the world showing police dogs and fire hoses being used by Police Chief Eugene "Bull" Connor against peaceful demonstrators in Birmingham, two black Protestant ministers in Danville led a demonstration at the municipal building. They were requesting equality in municipal employment, an end to school racial segregation, and desegregation of restaurants, hotels, and motels. Dorothy Miller began to tell Sam Shirah and me her story as we sat together in the basement office of the High Street Church. Dottie was small and stocky with shoulder-length brunette hair. She had a forthright manner. A practical young white woman from New York City, Dottie had a contagious laugh that broke easily and she liked to laugh at herself. She had already learned from working with Julian—as I would soon learn—to understate her descriptions. Yet, even though unadorned, her tale was gory.

The Reverend Lawrence Campbell and the Reverend Alexander I. Dunlap had decided to lead daily marches from May 31 to June 5, 1963, emphasizing the employment of black citizens. Dottie helped to make some of the demonstrators' signs; they had asked for jobs as firefighters, meter readers, police officers, secretaries, and clerks in municipal offices.

Shortly after the first march, the Commonwealth's attorney drew up an injunction against the key figures, and copied it, filling in the names of others who had marched. In short order, nearly two hundred people had been arrested for violating the injunction.

On June 5, according to Dottie's account, their patience wearing thin, the Reverend Mr. Campbell, the Reverend Mr. Dunlap, and several students asked to see Mayor Julian R. Stinson, who could not be found. The group said politely that they would wait and sat down on the floor. The police assaulted them, knocking the Reverend Mr. Dunlap down a flight of stairs and choking a young woman, who, forgetting her lessons in nonviolence, hit one of the policemen with her purse. Dottie burst into uncontrolled laughter at this part of the story, identifying with the young woman's exasperation and impatience shown by such a futile move. The young woman and the two clergymen were arrested, Dottie explained, the two ministers having been indicted by the grand jury for "inciting to riot" and "inciting or encouraging a minor to commit a misdemeanor," and bail was set at $5,500 for each. This was a high bail at that time.

The day after those arrests, June 6, was the day that the Reverend Mr. Campbell telephoned Jim Forman in Atlanta and fervently begged for help, saying that Danville was becoming another Birmingham. Jim sent the first field secretary to Danville on June 8; and another fourteen SNCC workers, including Dottie and me, were to follow throughout that summer.

A local newspaper, *The Roanoke Times,* editorialized on June 7:

Danville is now going through its ordeal of racial tension
brought on by those not content to rely upon the pro-
cedures of law to gain what they assert to be Negro
rights. The demonstrators have taken the issue out of the
courts and into the streets. . . . The Negroes of Danville
will have to realize that the only sound basis for obtaining the recognition they seek is by appeal to the
courts. . . . When any body of citizens takes it upon
themselves to determine which laws they will obey and
which they will defy we approach social anarchy.

Again the decision was made to march on the municipal
building, and on Monday afternoon, June 10, thirty-seven
individuals were arrested.

"Suddenly," Dottie said, her hands gesticulating, "police
officers snaked large coils of fire hoses into position on the
steps of the city hall. As the demonstrators continued walking, the fire hoses were turned on them full blast and police
started openly beating them with clubs."

That night, sixty-five black citizens—plus one lone
white SNCC worker, Dorothy Miller—walked five abreast
from the Bible Way Church to the city jail. Led by the
Reverend Hildreth G. McGhee, they sang hymns and cir-
cled the jail once, passing several impassive policemen. As
they began a second walk around, Chief of Police E. G.
McCain arrested twenty-four-year-old SNCC field secretary Bob Zellner, who had been photographing the demonstration (and whom Dottie would marry later that
August). The chief ordered the Reverend Mr. McGhee to
stop the singing. The minister instead passionately raised his
voice in a loud prayer for the police "who know not what
they do," and implored divine forgiveness for them. The
next thing Dottie knew, he was being led away by the police

and fire hoses were turned on full force toward those who remained. Police, including hurriedly deputized city employees, clubbed those who dodged under cars to escape the pressure of the fire hoses.

My father was the sixth minister in five generations of his Virginia and North Carolina family. I felt an irony in having been sent to Danville. Later that autumn, I wrote my English professor Benjamin Spencer at Ohio Wesleyan University, "I guess I felt a very real imperative to work in Danville."

When I mentioned to local reporters from the city's newspapers, *The Danville Register* and *The Bee,* my grandfather's ministry in Danville in the 1920s and my father's attendance at Stratford College, they sneered in disbelief and contempt. Their response revealed their lack of objectivity; it would have been easy for them to check my assertions. They simply didn't want to believe that a white with some connections to Danville would side with the "nigras." It was inconceivable to them. Yet my father's paternal family dates back to the seventeenth century in the five-county area around Danville on either side of the state line.

Those six ministers from the Danville area in five generations made me feel that I had a right to be there. Before my father, there was my grandfather, the Reverend William Luther King. His brother, Granville Booker King, and his half brother, Benjamin Cranford, were both ministers. My grandfather's first cousin William Sherman Epperson was an ordained Presbyterian minister and the son of John Epperson, who fought with the Union army during the Civil War and whose brother William Epperson was a Confederate soldier (such split loyalties were sometimes found in Southern families). The sixth was Wright Johnson.

There, in the south-central part of Virginia, about five miles from the North Carolina border, I felt close to my paternal great-grandmother, Justina Norman. She was the forebear who made the strongest impression on me when I was growing up. I pictured her as having a back as straight as a ramrod, perfect and proud carriage, and probing blue eyes. I have today her beautiful silver engraved watch, with its cornflower-blue enameled numbers, which still keeps time, and her brass thimble, which is the only one I use. I saw her in my mind as the sovereign of her family, stern, hardy, indomitable, but loving in her expressions and invincible in her faith. Born in 1850, she was eleven years old when the Civil War started. She once read the Bible through day by day and chapter by chapter, on her knees by a kerosene lamp. She had read the Bible in its entirety eighteen separate times, but "after that I lost count of how many times," she told my father. In the custom of her day, she kept a switch from a cherry tree by her side at the dining table, and any of her sons forgetting his manners would suddenly hear the swishing of the switch through the air and feel the sting of the thin cherry branch across the knuckles. Since my parents neither whipped nor hit me, I used to cringe when I thought of those cherry switches and their tender destinations and the more serious leather-belt whippings behind the woodshed for more grave infractions—like "talking back."

I am convinced that some of my tenacity comes from Justina Norman. Once I have made a decision and embarked on a goal, I proceed toward it much as she must have read the Bible on her knees, by sheer determination.

Justina Norman's father was Isaac Norman, a Methodist

lay preacher—a vital figure in the church societies of the rural areas of North Carolina and Virginia, where ordained ministers were scarce. Her three sons became ministers, one of those my grandfather. So strong was her faith that when my father, as a young man, in 1935, accompanied her up the aisle at the Petersburg funeral of another son, Granville, she looked down into the open coffin and instead of being swept away with grief, she smiled broadly and said, "I'll see you soon, son. I'll see you soon." Four years later, she died.

In this, however, I am unlike my great-grandmother, for I am still grappling with my mortality. The civil rights movement helped because it sharpened my focus on the issue of how I live rather than the question of how I die. But I have not yet achieved her peace of mind and acceptance of death.

My grandfather William Luther King was born at The Hollow (now Ararat) in Patrick County, Virginia, the second county west of Pittsylvania County, of which Danville was the largest town. With no public schools in the immediate post–Civil War period, obtaining an education was difficult in the isolated communities of the foothills of the Blue Ridge Mountains in Virginia. He was taught at the Friends Mission by Quaker missionaries who, with slender resources, educated him well. After graduating from a missionary school in Nyack, New York, now known as Nyack College, he was ordained as a Methodist minister. When he was assigned to Amherst County, Virginia, he rode horseback to the churches under his authority; in my favorite photograph of Pa King, as my brothers and I called him, he is seated on his horse, Lady, a four-gaited partner who took him from church to church.

Time moves slowly in such rural communities. Fifty-eight years after my grandfather had been assigned to another parish, my father drove up a mountain road in Amherst County looking for the Macedonia Methodist Church my grandfather had served. He asked two men sitting on a porch for directions, explaining, "My father was Preacher King." Peering at my father intently, one of the men responded, "I know you, Luther," as if nearly six decades had not passed. "How are your sister and brother, Esther and Norman?"

Pa King married a generous-spirited Presbyterian of Quaker heritage from Salem, New Jersey, Mary Ann Waddington. In 1897, when she was fourteen years old, my grandmother started keeping a diary. As I read it, she reminds me of myself, ravenously consuming books throughout her adolescence. On Friday, January 8, 1897, she wrote, "I finished *The Last Days of Pompeii* tonight"; five days later she had read *Little Women*. On January 24, she "ate hickory nuts and read the Bible all this afternoon." She was also like me in that she was able to assume responsibility very young. On January 29, "Miss Linda absent from school today because of snow. Only eleven pupils so the teacher asked me to take her classes and I did." This happened again on February 5: "Well, Miss Linda taught Miss Casper's room and I taught her room. I made out pretty well except getting a headache." On Tuesday, May 25, 1897, my grandmother turned fifteen, and wrote, "64° at 5:45 A.M. Weather clear. Today is my birthday. Aunt Han gave me five cents Saturday for my birthday and that is all the presents I received." Two months later she noted, "I gave $1 for the relief of the famine in India today"; this was a gargantuan sum for a fifteen-year-old considering the five cents she received for her birthday. My grandmother also could be a workhorse, as can I; elsewhere that year she mentions helping to mow seven loads of wheat one day, as well as threshing wheat and oats. One day in September she wrote, "We killed twenty-four pairs of chickens . . . receiving thirteen cents a pound." On December 1, she told her diary she was reading *Uncle Tom's Cabin*.

By the time she was training to become a teacher in "normal school," from which she was graduated in 1903, she showed herself to be even more like me in her concern for issues. These diaries reflect the way she wrestled with two looming questions of her day: evolution and the existence of the devil. She wrote each night of her discussions with other students and her teachers. On Sunday, January 11, 1903, she wrote, "I want to settle the question of my belief." The next day's entry read, "Effie says if her father thought I believed in the theory of evolution he would not let her go with me." On Friday, March 13, she penned, "I went over to school at 3 o'clock to hear a talk on settlement work in the slums." She wrote on April 3, "We went to the auditorium for an address by Booker T. Washington. It was very fine." She was a young woman concerned about the issues of her day as I would be a half-century later. April 11's entry read as follows: "This afternoon I . . . went around to Mr. Louderbough's, the Presbyterian minister at Salem. Had the long promised talk about evolution. Personally he does not accept the theory, he does believe in verbal inspiration, a personal devil and demoniacal possession."

On Saturday, May 9, she wrote, "My application for position of principal of the Hancock's Bridge School has been accepted at a salary of $38 a month." She often said that if she hadn't been a teacher, she would have been a lawyer, something to which few women then aspired. On May 19, she penned, "Started to read McCash's 'Religious Aspect of Evolution.'" The account for Monday, May 25, said, "Daisy Freeland was over this evening trying to make me give up the study of evolution." At approximately the period in my life when I was deliberating Albert Camus and the French existentialists, and considering my own religious doubts, she was weighing similar concerns. On Sunday, July 5, her entry read, "I didn't receive any help from the Communion. I don't know what I do believe or what I don't believe. I *do* believe in a God, other than that I do not know." The account for Wednesday, September 9, was significant: "Miss Harris introduced me to the new Methodist minister Mr. King this afternoon." He was my grandfather.

There was about my paternal grandparents a sense of peace and an unhurried grace that even now, when I think about them, casts a glow over whatever I am doing. My grandfather had a smile that came from deep within and I never saw him angry. My grandmother was warm and affectionate. They both had a quiet composure. Anger was alien to them; they tried instead to understand, to comprehend. I have sought to teach myself to react as they did, often without success. I have learned from them to attempt to understand hostile behavior. When I have been attacked behind my back, experienced the jealousy of others, or been undermined, I try hard not to react emotionally but to understand why people do as they do. Whether I comprehend it or not, I rarely waste time on vengeance.

As a child I went to "camp meetings" in the summer. My grandfather was the president of the ongoing yearly evangelical camp meeting in Spotsylvania County; I sat on the hard wooden benches of the "tabernacle" with my family as he preached and prayed, exhorting, and encouraging personal testimony. I don't know which had more lasting effect, my having been forced at a tender age to think about good and evil or my having learned discipline early from sitting straight for hours on bare pews.

It was my grandfather who awakened in my father his sense of justice, thereby influencing me. I have long thought that—had they known—my grandfather and grandmother would have been proud, despite the weight of the mores of their day, that I added my shoulder to the civil rights movement. My grandfather possessed something for which there is no other word but wisdom. He used to observe to my father while he was still a child that the idea of the Southern gentleman was often a myth. "Many a slave was more of a gentleman than his master," my grandfather observed during the early part of this century. When demagogues inveighed against "social equality" of the races and "race mixing" (along with "school mixing" and "job mixing," a favorite term of headline writers for Southern newspapers until the 1960s), my grandfather quietly said to my father that he thought that was very strange because obviously, judging from the ranges of skin color abundant in the South, there had been a great deal of "social equality" in the past.

It was Justina Norman King Cranford's grandfather, the Reverend Wright Johnson, who had walked 275 miles to Norfolk to be ordained and walked all the way back. The handwritten records of the Virginia Methodist Conference in the library of Randolph-Macon College at Ashland contain the documentation of his ordination. Saying grace was not enough; Wright Johnson knelt at the table to give thanks before meals and also used to get out of bed in the middle of the night to pray some more. Born in 1778, he preached until he was ninety years old. Then, in 1868, as he was walking along a country road, he suddenly threw up his hands in the air, looked heavenward, shouted "Glory!" and dropped dead.

In the way that families transmit values and blend memories of the past with daydreams of the future, creating a sense of potentiality, I feel Wright Johnson's influence on me— his pursuit of a cosmic dimension in ordinary life, his discipline, his firmness once he had made a decision, and his persistence. Perhaps Wright Johnson also unwittingly reinforced in me a feeling that my parents imparted to me— that there was special purpose for my life—when I learned that he used to pray, "God bless my children and my children's children and their children on down through the generations." I was going to need that.

My Grandmother Was a Great Person

By *Deidre Hair*

Ma, my grandmother, was not a great person. At least she wasn't the kind of person I studied in school. But then, nobody's grandmother is studied in school, right? Schools don't teach about people like my grandmother. History books don't have chapters on grandmothers. They don't even have pictures of Paul Revere's grandmother or Abraham Lincoln's grandmother. Some things have changed since I was a student, but even Women's Studies courses, to my knowledge, don't include "Readings in Great Grandmothers" or "Herstory: Grandmothers." To me, my grandmother was a great person, an average person who enjoyed making others feel great. Ma was, by the time of my childhood, a large, hardy lady, whose Methodist heritage forbade dancing . . . except in the depth and twinkle of her gray-green eyes. Oh, those eyes could dance, and one of the joys of my childhood was making them dance.

Alcohol was the spirit of the devil, Ma believed, and she was an authority, because the devil had come to earth to live

in the body of her father, my great-grandfather, who im-
bibed to extremes, and rarely remembered his behavior.
Not that he was evil or destructive. For example, while
philanthropy was not his habit, he once got so drunk that he
fixated on the ugliness of the local high-school band garb
and immediately purchased new uniforms for the entire
high-school band.

Ma was even and steady, and seemingly incapable of
emotional extremes. Her favorite expression was "Oh, my."
Whether Kellum's barn burned, or Smith's daughter was
getting married, or the neighbor's boy went off to Korea, or
I was accused of cutting Sunday school and spending my
offering money on a hot fudge sundae at the drugstore, her
reaction was always the same: "Oh, my." Cars were "machines" and, of course, she never wanted to drive one; she
didn't even like to ride in one. But once each year she
would ride in the machine to go to town for new shoes.

Her new shoes were always exactly like her old ones.
Sturdy, black, ground-gripping true-treads with long, thin
black laces. Shoes that could have been worn by the woman
who headed the orphanage in *Annie*. Shoes so serious they
made combat boots seem a trifle fashionable. They looked
terribly uncomfortable, with her pale, puffy ankles bulging
over the top of their rigid leather bindings. I remember
thinking that getting old meant all of your body fat heading
straight for your feet. I reasoned that if the fat ever reached
your feet, you would die. Why else would Ma wear her
shoes so tight? I knew the "fat" theory was true, because I
went to a funeral once, when I was eight years old, and you
could only see the top part of the deceased's body. His face
was much thinner than I had remembered. I was convinced
that the bottom portion of his body was concealed because
his feet were an embarrassment to the grieving family.

When I spent the night at Ma's house, I would worry that she would take her shoes off too soon before she lifted herself into bed. I didn't know how long it took for the fat to fall, but I knew that if her feet were up on the bed, the fat couldn't fall any lower and she couldn't die. That's all that mattered.

I never saw Ma in anything but a silky, small-flowered, static-ridden print dress. The print and the dress colors changed often, but the dress was always somehow the same. To me, she always looked like a grandmother, like the ones in children's books and Norman Rockwell paintings. She always cooked like a grandmother, too. Chuck roast with potatoes, onions, and carrots cooked in the same pan. Liver. Country-fried steak. Pork chops. Mashed potatoes. Green beans. Best of all, her fried chicken and white gravy every Sunday at noon. Noon, Sunday, fried chicken; there were no exceptions and there was no equal. She always said she couldn't make pie crust, but that was just another bit of Methodist modesty. Her pie crust was so good that I enjoyed strips of it baked with nothing on top but cinnamon 'n sugar.

After every meal at Ma's house, it was my job to take all the table scraps to the "patch" for burial. The patch was Ma's garden around the back of the house. All leftover food was buried about a foot deep and churned into the pitch-black soil. The garden had the best dirt in town, and I am sure it was the special white-gravy compost that provided a bountiful summer harvest. Of course, the odoriferous patch also attracted a variety of wild animals. But Ma was ready to defend her turf with her rusty, heavy, weather-beaten hoe, which was always close at hand.

At the age of seven, I ran away from home. It wasn't a big run because Ma lived six houses from my parents', and I wouldn't even consider running away to anyplace but Ma's house. My parents and I didn't see eye to eye, and I knew Ma would take me in. So I packed my suitcase (a large lunch pail) full of my stuffed animals, six-gun, and tie-down holster, put on my cowboy hat, announced my intention to run away forever to my parents, and went straight to Ma's to live the rest of my life in peace and without rules. My exit was far too hasty. I forgot my dog, Skipper. So I had to go back and once again announce my definite, defiant departure.

Skipper and I arrived at Ma's just in time for supper. Ma promised she wouldn't tell my parents where I was, and she said I could stay at her house as long as I helped with the chores. One big chore was to pick up sticks all over the yard. It was a big yard, full of mature trees and mature tree droppings. For every two hours of work, I would receive a quarter. In two days I had saved one dollar. That doesn't really tell you how much I worked, though, for Ma lived only two blocks from the drugstore, and I really did have a weakness for those hot fudge sundaes. I gave serious thought to using my saved dollar to go to Texas on a Greyhound bus, but then I wasn't really sure if I could find the Long Ranger once I got there. Ma said she'd heard that the Long Ranger had moved to Nevada because the air was much better than in Texas, so I just decided to play it safe and stay put at her house until I had enough money to go to both Texas and Nevada. Besides, living at Ma's was like going to heaven. My pesky older sisters weren't around to nag me, hit me, or blame things on me, and at Ma's house I had unlimited playtime and unrivaled attention. No question about it . . . I was Ma's favorite.

Ma had two doting sons and a kindly carpenter husband who truly believed that idle hands were the devil's workshop. He rarely spoke, but he was always deeply involved in some sort of "project." All three of her grandchildren were girls, and I was the youngest. When the others would pick on me, she would come to my rescue. "Don't you worry if they call you ugly. Just remember that ugly children grow up to be beautiful." It was a curious thing for her to say, since I never really thought I was an ugly child . . . no matter what my sisters said. Besides, playing baseball and cowboys was far more important to me than being "beautiful."

During my four-day runaway stay at Ma's place, some of my clothes miraculously appeared in a sack in my room. Had she told my parents where I was? Was she capable of such treachery? From that point on, I listened to all of her phone conversations from a secret perch at the top of the stairs as she stood in the front hallway, which separated the two parlors. She was slightly hard of hearing, so even her whisper was easily decoded. "It's not working, she wants to stay for good." "Skipper's fine, but he chewed my slippers last night." "Okay, after work tomorrow." Yep, she was a double agent, and "after work tomorrow" was exactly when my parents came to Ma's and took me home.

For punishment, I was not allowed to play outside with my best friends, two other baseball-playing cowboys named Charlie and Smoky, for one whole day. I was grounded. But it was a day spent deep in vengeful thought. The next day Charlie, Smoky, and I acted out my plan. We got our bikes and rode past Ma's house as fast as we could, throwing sticks into the yard without ever slowing down or looking back. By dusk, our mission was complete, and her big yard was a mess. That would show her!

Later that same week, we went to Ma's yard to play ball. She was in the front of her creek-stone porch, thrusting her heavy hoe into the ground again and again, like a woman possessed. She was killing a family of snakes that had taken up residence under the porch. She told us to go around the back of the house until she finished. I saw one snake split in half, and I wanted to watch, but I sensed that she was in no mood for disobedience.

We ran to the back of the house and began to wrestle in the yard. Ma came around the corner of the house just in time to see Charlie throw me to the ground. "Charlie, what's the matter with you? You don't hit girls! Ever. You do that again, and I'm gonna take this hoe to you . . . just like those snakes." Charlie was terrified, and he didn't hit me for at least a week. But it was okay for me to whomp him, because there was no rule that girls couldn't hit boys.

Ma had recaptured a place in my heart. She also paid me to remove the sticks that had blown into the yard after that terrible summer storm . . . that storm that had never happened. After that week, we were fast friends again, and we never tried to teach each other any lesson except love.

My Grandmother

❦

By Ruth Rambo

There are many areas in which you can experience disadvantage. Oh! You can be economically disadvantaged (live on the Gold Coast instead of the Platinum one) or intellectually disadvantaged (attend Harvard instead of Fisk or Morehouse) or physically disadvantaged (be a woman of color with snake hips) or even culturally disadvantaged (have never heard B.B. King sing, or play "Lucille").

My brother and I were grandparentally disadvantaged. We knew only one—our maternal grandmother, Mrs. Annie B. Scott Mitchell, whom we were encouraged to call "Grandmother Mitchell," a practice that I found enormously confusing. It would have made a great deal of sense to me as a child if we had known "Grandmother Rambo," whose very existence and certainly whose availability would have required us to use some distinguishing language. We would need to say "Grandmother Rambo" to set her apart from Grandmother Mitchell. But there was no other grandmother. For that matter, there was no other grandparent. We were at the same time grandfather deprived as well, suffering an absolute void of male grandparentness. So on two counts, there was no need for that much clarity. We had one grandmother, so why add her last name, and since there were no male grandparents, why even bother to call her Grandmother? It seemed like one of those irrational and unreasonable things that adults force children to do. We didn't need to be that specific to summon one tiny little snow-haired lady. We could have called her Grand or we could have called her Granny or we could have called her Grandma, but we were told to call her Grandmother Mitchell. We did as directed.

Actually, we were only technically grandparentally disadvantaged. Grandmother Mitchell did the work of four and did it well. She was up to it because she was competent. Today's youth might say she was fierce, but Grandmother Mitchell forbade the use of slang or idiomatic expressive language. She had been born before the turn of the century, when only the most perfect English was spoken by the black (I think we were Negroes then) bourgeois. Grandmother Mitchell was nothing if not middle class. She herself had attended and finished college and married a mailman—I mean, a postal carrier—who was also the head of the Knights of Pythias. Did I mention that she was the brightest, most worshipful Eastern star in the firmament? She couldn't have been any more middle class than that. I don't know the details of the courtship and romance of Annie B. Scott and Lewis Mitchell, Sr., but I suspect that she chose him and one evening he found himself on bended knee proposing.

That was the one big thing I appreciated about our grandmother: she was competent. Our grandmother could do all that stuff that everybody else's grandmother could do. She had the cleanest floors, the sparklingest silver, the fluffiest pillows this side of the Rio Grande. And, if it doesn't sound like bragging or even if it does, my grand-mother did it better. Yes! She did.

There was this time that I wanted a pretty pink dress for Easter. So we went to the department store to see the dress I wanted—right there in the window of a major downtown department store in Austin, Texas. She didn't go inside the store. She was much too shrewd for that because shopping in the stores for any black person (bourgeois or not) in the South was very troublesome in those days—almost as diffi-cult as shopping in the urban North is today for black male teens. So she didn't bother to go inside the store to look at the dress or feel the material or check the seams or the sleeves. No. Not Grandmother Mitchell. She stood, trouble-free, on the sidewalk outside the store looking through the glass at this pretty pink dress. On a scrap of paper she made a few scribbles, unintelligible to me, and then went home. She went home and demonstrated her competence. No, that's not right, she performed magic.

Instead of waving a wand, she cut some brown-paper grocery bags into some strangely shaped pieces and taped them together. I don't remember ever being involved in the process. I don't think she measured me or tried it on me during any of the steps. Actually, I don't think I was allowed in the room while that Singer was whirling and she was muttering—probably some incantation or another. I do remember, though, that I was without question the best-dressed eight-year-old in Austin on that Easter Sunday morning. I can still feel the silky quality of the fabric and the texture of the lace decorating the neck, sleeves, and hem of my garment. It was an act of magic, and I knew then that her ability to make this dress—prettier than the one in the store window—made her a witch.

If memory serves, I think my big mouth once uttered the

word *witch* as a descriptor of the competent Grandmother Mitchell. (If my memory storage system is vague on this point, that part of my anatomy that graciously allows me to sit in a chair has a very strong and clear recollection of the incident.) The word I used was *witch,* and rarely have I been more correct. That was actually not my meaning at the time, but prophetic nonetheless. She excelled competence, she performed magic.

Then there was the matter of my baldness. When I was two, according to family accounts and photographs, I had the hair of a newborn. When I had reached four, I would show these pictures with the explanation: "This is a picture of me when I was a little boy." My hair follicles would not cooperate with the family expectations for growth. So while I was expected to have at least a full head of good hair, not only did I not have "good" hair like my grandmother, I had very little "bad" hair. It was hard to make an assessment of its quality, for there was so little of it to judge. Our grandmother set out to handle this challenge.

Grandmother Mitchell went into the kitchen and closed the door—her version of a DO NOT DISTURB sign—and created this hair-growing poultice. I think it included castor oil (she seemed real fond of that), lanolin, mineral oil (another favorite presented for internal consumption), and some other potions. She combined these ingredients into a hair pomade, which she routinely rubbed into my scalp and which was followed by a very vigorous brushing. This regimen continued twice daily for many months. There is nothing so fundamental to the bonding of a grandmother and granddaughter than sitting on the floor with your shoulders held in a vise grip while your grandmother vigorously brushes your scalp. Remember, there was very little hair there to be brushed. But in time, this competent cosmetician had created thick, long hair to brush and tend. An assessment was made that it was neither good nor bad hair. It was merely *hair,* and she was happy that it was thick so when it was straightened and oiled, I would look presentable.

When I complained of the discomfort attendant to transforming my hair into good hair, she countered with this thought: "The road to beauty knows no pain." I had enormous respect for her skills, but I didn't believe everything she said. I should have 'cause she was, after all, exceptional, smart, *and* competent.

Captain Mary B. Greene

By L. Jane Greene

Shortly after a Bicentennial committee erected a statue of my grandmother, a reporter found her way to my door and asked a million questions, most of which I didn't know the answers to. After all, I was only eight when Grandma died. For instance, when Newspaper Lady asked me why my grandmother chose to be a steamboat captain in a day when women simply didn't do that, I flippantly replied, "It was either that or swim." I thought that was pretty funny, in spite of the criticism it elicited from family and friends. They would have preferred that I romanticize her reasons, paint her in Mark Twain hues, suggest that she was lured to the river by the haunting blows of the steamboat whistle. The fact is that Mary Becker Greene married a steamboat captain and owner, Captain Gordon C. Greene. If she was to remain in his company, she would have to be on board one of the steamboats that he navigated. In short, she studied the river, became a pilot, and got a captain's license. She was the only woman in the early 1900s with the title of steamboat captain.

Captain Mary's career elicited national attention. Eventually, crowds of river fans sought her autograph. Seekers would cock their heads as they gazed upon Captain Mary's modest smile, while she scribbled her name on the backs of menus or books. As she accrued brave deeds, admiration for her heightened. She had survived floods, hurricanes, and cyclones on her steamboat journeys. During one flood, my grandfather died aboard one of his steamboats. Grandma, honoring his request to be taken to his resting place by boat, ignored the crew's insistence that going upriver to Marietta would be dangerous. Too dangerous. "Too dangerous, my foot!" she protested. And to Marietta they went, by steamboat, with Grandma at the helm and Grandpa "on ice" until they got there. Gutsy!

Her most notable heroism, in my eyes, was her sincere affection for humanity. She loved people, a fact that attracted passengers to take myriad repeat steamboat trips. They called her "Captain Mary," "Ma Greene," "Mary B.," or "Mamie," all depending on how well they knew her. She greeted passengers from every walk of life as if they were kinfolk, kissing them right on the chops and fussing over them as if they were mischievous children ready to perform in a school concert.

Her passenger fans and friends would bring her gifts, such as decks of cards, Depression glass, pictures of themselves. She would pile these gifts on the top bunk in her stateroom, a habit that made my daddy crazy. A steamboat captain himself and the heir to their company, Greene Line Steamers, he'd say to his mother, "Ma, why don't you throw some of this junk outa here?!" She would insist that it wasn't junk, as she relished every gift that the passengers brought her. When she'd launch into the history behind every trinket, my dad would take off, leaving Captain Mary in the midst of her memories.

Captain Mary went out of her way to make people smile. For instance, if she saw little boys on shore, would-be Tom Sawyers waving and jumping around in glee to see a steamboat paddle by, she'd tell the pilot to pull over and let the kids come on board for a ride up to the next dam. The kids might even be allowed to steer the boat, an experience they would never forget.

So far, I've been reminiscing about the public grandma, the steamboat oddity. But how did she relate to her grandchildren? To me, she was the Queen of Laughter and the one whom I could depend on to spoil me rotten. How I loved it when she returned from a steamboat trip to New Orleans, her suitcases gorged with pralines, dolls, and strings of beads that she'd purchased in the Quarter. After the commotion of greetings died down, Grandma would entertain us with hilarious stories about her journeys, proving that "Old Man River" laughs when he keeps on "rollin' along." As we grew, she'd stare at us with a gaze that not only looked but *saw*. Her blue eyes, set like jewels in her Santa Claus face, had a clarity of vision that made one feel that she could read a mind or see into the future. The wrinkles around her eyes were rays of kindness. She always set her mouth at a half smile, as if waiting for the punch line, and when she laughed, she'd rip off her wire-rimmed glasses and wipe the tears from her jovial eyes. Her laughter was genuine rather than a filler for an awkward silence. I never saw her get angry, although I'd heard others, particularly Daddy, refer to her "fits." "Don't do this or that because Grandma will have a fit." I only saw fits of laughter.

On Arbor Day of 1949, the school gave us baby trees to take home and plant. What a beautiful sunny day it was when my brother Tom and I planted our tree, packed it down, and watered it. Afterward, Mother called us inside to tell us the bad news. Grandma had died. Eighty years old and never a sick day. Just went into her stateroom on *The Delta Queen* to take her nap and never woke up. Dazed, I, at that moment, developed Grandma's stare, which sees rather than merely looks. Sadness fashions it.

The tree we planted that day still exists, except now it's wide, very, very tall, and its boughs could probably hold up a whole slew of "Tom Sawyers."

A Different Kind of Starch

By *Elizabeth Isele*

My grandfather used to call her "Little Pistol." Nana was barely five feet tall. She wore a size-three shoe, and that was only after she married and had two children. Before then, she wore a size one. Her shoes had to be custom-made.

All Nana's clothes were custom-made, too, in beautiful colors and exquisitely textured fabrics. Hats (half-veiled), dresses, shoes, stockings, handbags, and gloves—everything matched. She always wore gloves. Cotton in summer and suede in winter: the softest suede I ever felt. As passionately as she loved dressing up, she always told me, "It's not the clothes but what's underneath that counts."

Her childhood home, a brownstone in New York City, was furnished with English antiques and Oriental carpets. Oil paintings hung in gold frames on silk-covered walls. Warm gaslight and music filled the rooms and there were servants to cook, clean, polish silver, do laundry, groom the horses, shovel out stalls, oil hand-tooled carriages, light the fires in winter, and ladle lemonade for the ice man in summer.

When Nana was ten she demanded a cart for Banjo, her favorite pony. From that time on, instead of riding in an elegant carriage through Central Park with her parents, her beautiful older sister, and handsome younger brother, she took up the reins and rode in her pony cart.

Every Sunday morning she gave Banjo a flick of the whip and they streaked out after the family carriage. Back and forth—first behind, then alongside, then in front—Nana and Banjo raced along like lunatics. Her mother was appalled.

"She is really quite a handful," her mother decided, and sent Nana off to private schools, hoping they might make a "lady" of her. The schools had stodgy names like Miss Porter's and Emma Walker's, and Nana was bored there.

"Art history, manners, and deportment," she said, remembering the curriculum with disgust. "What good are grace and decorum if you can't have any fun?"

Her last year of formal education was at Chalfonte-Haddon Hall, a "finishing school." "Finish, my foot," she said. "I have hardly begun."

That fall, she met my grandfather at a Halloween costume ball. She had come dressed as a milkmaid and he as a farmer. Nana said, "We started dancing that night and never stopped."

His family was not at all sure Nana was the right woman for their son to marry. They were strict Methodists and Nana's family were Lutherans. Lutheran was synonymous with libertine to them, and Nana was, after all, Nana.

Her family, however, was delighted. They felt marriage might be just the thing to calm Nana down. I don't think it calmed down either one of them. I met my grandfather for the first time on an August afternoon so hot that the air shimmered above our driveway. I had been waiting hours for them on the front porch and raced down to meet their long, black Packard. My grandfather stepped out first, wearing a seersucker suit and tie, shiny shoes, and a Panama hat with a blue-and-white band to match his suit. I had expected a farmer; I hadn't realized he would be just as custom-made as Nana.

He was so tall, I could not see his face. He reached out his arm to me, scooped me up close, and smiled. With his other hand he pulled an ice cream cone from behind his back. "For you," he said. "I hope you like chocolate."

"We're driving out West," said Nana. "We want to see the prairie and the deserts, ghost towns and old gold mines, and cowboys and Indians, if there are any left."

Nana sent me picture postcards with hastily scribbled notes such as "On the trail in Santa Fe" and "Beautiful turquoise jewelry here in New Mexico." Grandpa took her picture next to a giant cactus in Arizona, and they mailed an envelope full of buffalo hair from Wyoming. Nana learned how to weave from a Navajo woman in Taos, and they barreled down treacherous dirt roads in Colorado in hot pursuit of some cowpuncher's chuck wagon. She didn't much like branding steers at the roundup, but Nana loved panning for gold outside of Sacramento.

They tied a burlap water bag over the front of the radiator and drove the Packard through Death Valley. In a ghost town, they had someone take their picture in front of the saloon. Grandpa looked a little self-conscious in his sheepskin chaps and ten-gallon hat. Nana's cowboy boots were so big she appeared somewhat wobbly, and her ten-gallon hat squished the tops of her ears, but she was beaming.

When I listened to the "Lone Ranger" on our old Philco radio, I pictured my grandmother charging over the hills after desperados shouting, "Hi, ho, Banjo, away!"

She sent me cowboy boots and a pair of six-shooters with

red and green leather holsters. I wore them morning, noon, and night. My mother was aghast. Finally, after months on the road, they came back East for Christmas. We were waiting at their house when they drove in. The Packard looked a little worse for wear, but Nana looked grand. Still wearing her cowboy hat, she had attached a little half-veil to it for the holidays.

On Christmas Eve Nana taught me how to string popcorn and cranberries for her tree. We sat on the big down sofa—the one whose pillows were plumped at least three times a day. At the other end of the living room, Grandpa played Christmas carols on the Victrola for my brother and sister. The draperies were open just enough for us to see frost etching the windowpanes.

My mother, Nana's daughter, was not back yet. Someone had telephoned from the station bar, and she had gone out looking for my father. Sometimes she found him, most times she didn't.

I never knew my mother well. I still don't. She felt children should be seen and not heard. Appearances were important to her, and she wanted us to be "seen" perfectly. We were scrubbed and starched. Even our underwear was starched. She had some peculiar economies. One of them was recycling our old sheets by making them into underpants for my sister and me. Actually they looked more like boxer shorts, so she sewed eyelet lace around the legs. I hated them.

Above all, we were to be quiet. Sometimes my mother spent the entire day in her bedroom with the shades drawn. She had terrible headaches, and my thundering around the house in my cowboy boots firing caps from my six-shooters did not help. Her silences frightened me, and I was desperate for some sound—even my own.

I heard the pantry door swing open and Frances, Nana's

cook, carried hot cinnamon cider and warm cocoa into the living room. We smelled her Christmas stollen and gingerbread cookies baking in the kitchen. "Soon," she said.

Sitting close to Nana, I tried not to scratch where my starched underwear itched. We were watching Grandpa clip the candles onto the tree, when suddenly a bolt of lightning ripped into the old beech tree beside the house. The bolt ricocheted off the tree and burst through the window by the sofa. It shot across the living room past the Victrola and out the window directly opposite the one it had entered. I was terrified. Nana hugged me tight and said, "My goodness! We almost didn't have to light the candles on the tree this year, did we?"

It had nothing to do with the lightning, but my grandfather died shortly after that Christmas. Nana missed him terribly. She said, "It's all these trappings. I just can't find him in all these trappings."

She decided to move to California—not to Death Valley or to Gold Rush territory, but to a little beach house they had seen together in Santa Monica. "I can picture you carting a few things across country in a covered wagon and settling down here by the water," Grandpa had said.

When she came to say good-bye, Nana's arms were loaded with big boxes. "Wait downstairs," she said as she struggled through my bedroom door.

Finally she called and I bolted upstairs. Clothes were carefully arranged all over my bed. She had put a hat on my pillow. There was a beautiful blue-and-white dress, and a purse and matching shoes with light blue socks tucked inside. And lying next to all of this were six pairs of soft Carters underpants with ponies printed all over them. "For a very special cowgirl," she said, reaching out to touch my cheek. "With love from Nana."

When it was time to go to college, I chose one in California. My mother and father thought I was crazy. "One year," they said. "We'll pay for one year, and then you'll come back East, where you belong."

I never came home again. I spent many school holidays with Nana at the beach house. The Christmas Eve when she was seventy-four we opened presents around a tabletop tree with tiny candles on it. She looked at me and said, "How about New Year's in Alaska? I'd like to hear more about that Iditerod."

The Sunday Dinner
That Got Away

By *Margra Hyde*

I have many memories of my grandmother, and this incident is just one of them.

There were certain rules she adhered to. One of them
was on raising and preparing chickens for the dinner table.
A chicken was never to be caught up from the yard and
eaten without first being cooped for at least two weeks or
longer. Her explanation: a chicken eats anything and
everything—snails, lizards, even snakes. So they must have
a cleansing period.

She never kept a rooster; the henhouse didn't need a boss.
There were bantams and broody hens for eggs. The eggs
that we ate were purchased from a neighbor. Once when
she bought a sitting of eggs, the neighbor included, for free,
a very large egg, saying he had no idea where it came from
but that it was probably a goose egg and might not hatch. It
did hatch and was a very large chick. Sex: a rooster. This
was in late summer, so the rooster was around till the next
spring. By this time he was taking over the roost. So my

grandmother said, "He has to go." The rooster was cooped; then came the Saturday for his demise.

Someone new enters my story: my dad, who was to be the executioner. Usually there wasn't any problem, but this time there was. The rooster refused to lie still and keep his head on the chopping block. At last, he finally seemed settled, so Dad brought the axe down and tossed the bird onto the grass to bleed.

Evidently the axe had only stunned him, for the rooster got to his feet, staggered a few steps, and took to the air. He cleared our neighbor's barn and kept on flying. The last we saw of him was a white spot against the sky.

While I'm watching our Sunday dinner fly away and thinking, *No chicken and dumplings for Sunday dinner,* Dad is standing behind me and the air is blue with words I've never heard before; words not fit for the ears of a child of my tender years.

While all this was happening, my grandmother was waiting near the back steps with hot water and the plucking tub, ready for the next step in preparing Mr. Rooster for the pot. As we watched the rooster disappear, Grandmother dropped to the steps and started to laugh. She laughed until tears rolled down her cheeks. Every time she started to get to her feet, she looked at my dad and said, "Oh, my goodness," and began to laugh again.

This was the one and only time I ever saw her lose control of her emotions, for my grandmother was a lady, very dignified and grand in the Southern tradition of lady-like behavior. This was the first time I realized that even ladies could be human enough to forget that they are ladies.

I do not know if this is a story about the Sunday dinner that got away or a story about my grandmother. I will leave it to you to decide.

My French Great-Grandmother

By Dorothy A. Schueler

Louise Prax, my great-grandmother, was born in the Alsace-Lorraine section of France in 1837. The little five-foot-two charmer was called Nana by her family. It always intrigued us that she wore seven petticoats. I never did learn why, other than to pad her slim figure.

It was usual in those days to arrange marriages between a daughter and an eligible young man. Nana's mother had a sister living in New York City and she just happened to know a young Frenchman for Louise. So off Nana went on a sailing ship to meet her future husband.

During the journey an epidemic broke out, and Nana and a handsome young man were the only passengers to escape the illness. It was their duty, they felt, to help care for the ailing passengers. The rest is history. Louise and François Pellegrin fell in love. Upon arriving in New York, Nana's future bridegroom was given the sad news. But Louise and François rejoiced.

Their marriage produced thirteen children, but only the firstborn, my grandmother, and the last one survived. We don't know at what age François died, but at that time

Nana's two children were married and being a very independent person, she sold her home for $2,500 and entered a retirement home for respectable elderly women. She was fifty-two years old and lived there happily until her death at ninety-five. The home, you can guess, didn't make any money from her.

Could Nana return to this earth, she would be surprised to learn that the small auxiliary comprising about twenty-five women had grown in such size and wealth that they were able to purchase a large hotel in the Orange Mountains. They furnished it with beautiful antiques, including a huge Waterford chandelier for the lobby.

The $2,500 my great-grandmother paid for admission in those days would probably just cover the monthly maintenance plus the very large entrance fee today. Needless to say, it is now a very classy residence.

Each time we visited Nana, she would insist upon taking us to her various friends in each of their rooms. Without introducing us by name she would say, "This is my great-grandaughter, and these are my great-great-grandchildren."

Mama Dear

By *Yolande Giovanni*

We lived in Knoxville, Tennessee. I was born in Albany, Georgia, as were my sisters, Anna Elizabeth and Agnes Marjorie. Mother, Daddy, Mama Dear, and we girls moved to Knoxville when Daddy took a teaching position at Austin High School. My grandmother, Mama Dear, has always been a part of my life. Mother said that once, when I was a baby, Mama Dear (who lived with us) went to visit her daughter, Willard, and I missed her and grieved so for her that I got sick. I had what started off as flu and then it went to double pneumonia, and Mother was real worried that I was going to die. I don't remember that, of course, but Mother always said that I got sick because I missed Mama Dear so much.

Mama Dear told us that she was a free child of slave parents. And the people who owned her parents taught her to read and write. She wasn't supposed to, but she knew how to read and write. A lot of black children didn't know how. And then before Anna and I started school, she taught us to read and to spell. When Anna was four and I was five, Mother said it was time for us to go to school. They didn't have kindergarten then. But there was a Presbyterian school, and Mother took us there and they accepted us. I forget what the tuition was, something like fifty cents a week.

After we started school and Mama Dear was getting up in age, Daddy told her to quit working. She was working in a high-school cafeteria and Mother started working over there. For a while they both worked there and then Mama Dear quit working and stayed at home. She was the one who used to clean us up after school. She would comb my hair and Anna's hair, too. She had to wrap it. She used to take black thread to keep it braided. My hair was very fine.

Mama Dear let us know that we had to get out of the house and do something. Once, I remember that Agnes, our baby sister, took my shoestrings and put her broken ones in my shoes. I didn't want to go to school with an ugly old broken shoelace, so I announced that I wasn't going. And Mama Dear said, "Girl, you're going somewhere." She never struck any of us, but she had a way of looking at you that put the fear of God in you. I was scared to death to make her upset.

We lived across the street from Cal Johnson Park. The water fountain was directly in front of our front porch, though you had to cross Mulvaney Street to get to it. The kids used to take their hands and turn the water on and squirt it on people. There was this little boy who went and got a mouthful and spewed it on me. Mama Dear was sitting on the porch and she said, "Hey, you! You stay right there. I'm gonna get a bucket of water and drown you." Mother almost cracked up. She said, "Mama Dear, what do you think that boy is going to do while you go in the house and get a bucket of water?" The things Mama Dear told you to do—you just did! And the little boy didn't have sense enough to know he could just run away. But she didn't throw the water. She just scared him half to death.

Another time, we went to a program at Mt. Zion Baptist Church, and Mama Dear paid for all of us to go to it. It didn't cost much, maybe a penny apiece. During the program, she had to take one of us out—I think it was Agnes—but anyway, when she came back in, whoever was taking tickets said, "Where's your ticket, Mrs. Watson?" And she said, "I already paid." She wasn't about to pay again. Like when you go to a racetrack and they stamp your hand, she wouldn't have let them stamp anything on her. Why? Because she paid, and if she had to go out, she had to go out and she wasn't going to pay again. She was very determined. She was a kindhearted person, but she was very set in her ways about things.

Her birthday was November 24, and one particular year it fell on Thanksgiving Day; Mother had planned a surprise party. Mama Dear got up that morning and she was real upset because Mother didn't have turkey, she wasn't doing anything. And Mama Dear asked, "Aren't you fixing anything for Thanksgiving?" And Mother said, "I'm thankful for everything I've got every day; I don't have to be thankful one particular day just because the white folks are." Mama Dear was furious, but she didn't say anything. She always wore dresses that had lace collars that were detachable. She would wash and starch and iron them and wear them when she was going to church or the lodge. And this particular day she put her collar on and her hat and took her purse and stormed out of the house. We were too little to know what was going on; we didn't know anything about surprise parties. But I know Mother had turkey and stuff hidden all over the neighborhood. When Mama Dear came back, she said, "I could see we weren't having Thanksgiving here, so I had it at the church." She had had a turkey dinner at the church, but later that evening people started coming in and she was so surprised that Mother was having this birthday party for her. I remember she was real happy. I don't remember the gifts or anything, but I know people brought her things. She must have been old then.

I remember that she used to take Anna and me uptown. Agnes was still a baby. Mama Dear would get ready to go to town and we would say, "Mama Dear, let us go," and she would say, "Come on, come on." And then one time we decided to take our dolls and our buggies. She didn't say anything. She said very little. We went through Cal Johnson Park around to the Clint Street Bridge. It was wooden. When we got to the bridge, I looked down and saw the water and I couldn't move. I had walked across there many a time, but I guess with the doll buggy I thought I would fall in. Mama Dear had walked on across, and there I stood. She kept saying, "Come on." And she finally came back and got me. "That's the last time I'll take you with me, you can stay at home. You bring all this junk." She just fussed. But we went on uptown and a lot of white people used to see us and they would ask whoever was with us, "Are they twins?" Just because we were little girls almost the same age. Anna was a year and a day younger than I, but we never did look alike. Mama Dear would get so mad. Anna and I laughed. Are we twins? I remember she bought us mittens—that's before we graduated to gloves—to wear to school. We went into the bakery shop and she bought us ladyfingers. I've loved ladyfingers ever since.

Mama Dear always kept peppermint in her trunk in her room. Daddy kept his trunk on the back porch and so did Mother, but Mama Dear's was in her room. She always had a gigantic barber pole. I guess she kept them from

Christmas to Christmas. She had a little cobbler's hammer, and if she wanted to reward us or if we pleased her, she would go chip off a piece of peppermint. My daughter Nikki says she remembers Mama Dear's peppermint, but I don't see how she can. She was only three or four when Mama Dear died. But Nikki loves peppermint, too.

Mama Dear used to make apple jelly and keep it in the bedroom trunk because she didn't want anyone to eat it. You had to ask her for it. She could do more with an apple than anybody I've ever seen. She'd peel it and make an apple tart. She would boil the peelings and make apple jelly and with some of the apples she'd make applesauce, and then she'd make more apple jelly. She used everything in the apple except the seeds. We always had plenty of apple jelly and apple pies. That was before refrigerators. You had iceboxes. She'd make the apple pies and you'd just have to eat them. I don't care for any berry—not blackberry, blueberry, strawberry—none of them. Those little berries get in your teeth or stain your hands or just, well, I don't care for berries. But applesauce, apple butter, apple pie—I can eat them every day.

Contributors

Mildred Andrews earned a bachelor's degree in education from Radford University and a master's degree from Virginia Tech. For many years Mrs. Andrews taught English, Latin, and history in public schools throughout Virginia. Since 1987 she has been residing in the Showalter Center of Warm Hearth Village Retirement Community in Virginia.

Kathleen Carroll Bailey Angle is a teacher, writer, and photographer with twenty-five years' experience in college and public-school teaching. A native of Virginia who received her Ph.D. from Indiana University of Pennsylvania, she is currently a language arts teacher at Frank W. Cox High School in Virginia Beach.

Gwendolyn Brooks was born in Topeka, Kansas, but has lived most of her life in Chicago. Since the publication of her first book of poetry in 1943, she has received many awards and honors for her work, including two Guggenheim fellowships and the first Pulitzer Prize for poetry awarded to an African-American.

Daryl Cumber Dance is professor of English at the University of Richmond, Virginia. She is the author of a number of books, including *Shuckin' and Jivin': Folklore from Contemporary Black Americans; Long Gone: The Mecklenburg Six and the Theme of Escape in Black Folklore;* and *New World Adams: Conversations with Contemporary West Indian Writers.*

Sharon Dilworth, author of *The Long White,* was the recipient of the Iowa Short Fiction Award. She teaches at Carnegie-Mellon University in Pittsburgh.

Anna Esaki-Smith was reared in Westchester County, New York, the daughter of Japanese immigrants. She wants readers to know that although for many years she tried to be as all-American as she could, she has begun to realize the value of her heritage and to treasure the memories of her grandmothers. She lives with her husband in Hong Kong.

Virginia C. Fowler, a native of Lexington, Kentucky, was educated at the University of Kentucky and the University of Pittsburgh. An associate professor of English at Virginia Tech, she is the author of two books, *Henry James's American Girl* and *Nikki Giovanni,* and the editor of *Conversations with Nikki Giovanni.*

Arlynn S. Geers grew up in St. Louis, Missouri, and currently lives in Warm Hearth Village Retirement Community in Virginia. She travels often and is Warm Hearth's "window on the world."

Yolande Giovanni was born in Albany, Georgia, the oldest of three daughters. After earning her B.A. in history from Knoxville College in Knoxville, Tennessee, she married and had two daughters—Gary Ann and Nikki. Ms. Giovanni's piece in this collection is a tribute and memorial to her grandmother, Cornelia Warren Watson, who played a great part in rearing her and her sisters.

L. Jane Greene grew up traveling up and down inland rivers on her family's steamboat. An English teacher at Withrow High School in Cincinnati, Ohio, she holds a master's degree in English from Xavier University.

Deidre Hair is a judge in Cincinnati and the author of *No Shoes. No Shirt. No Trial.*

Margra Hyde is a resident of the Warm Hearth Retirement Home, and is a member of the Warm Hearth Writers Workshop.

Elizabeth Isele has been involved in book publishing for almost thirty years. The former manager of the T. Y. Crowell and J. B. Lippincott juvenile imprints of Harper & Row, Ms. Isele is the author of nine books for young readers. In addition to running her own complete literary services firm, she teaches creative writing at Wesleyan University.

Anna W. Kenney was born in 1902 in Chatham, Virginia. She went on to receive her B.A. from the College of William and Mary, and eventually to become curator at Smithfield Plantation in Blacksburg, Virginia. She lives in Warm Hearth Village Retirement Community.

Mary King has served in several capacities in government and was a senior-level official in the Carter administration.

Since her civil-rights days, she has traveled to seventy-seven developing countries, dealing directly with issues such as international trade and commercial relations with the Third World. She lives in Washington, D.C., with her husband, psychiatrist and author Peter G. Bourne.

Maxine Hong Kingston is the author of a number of highly acclaimed books, including *The Woman Warriors: Memoirs of a Girlhood Among Ghosts; China Men;* and *Tripmaster Monkey: His Fake Book.*

Doris Moore traveled throughout the country as a secretary for the Tax Court of the United States. Since 1989 she has lived in Warm Hearth Village Retirement Community in Virginia, enjoying the people and the history she has learned from them.

Kyoko Mori was born in Kobe, Japan, and has lived in the American Midwest since 1977. She is the author of the novel *Shizuko's Daughter;* a book of poetry, *Fallout;* and short stories that have appeared in *The Kenyon Review, The American Scholar,* and other journals.

Gloria Naylor is a writer for theater, film, and television and the author of a number of award-winning novels, including *Women of Brewster Place; Linden Hills;* and *Bailey's Cafe.* Ms. Naylor has received both Guggenheim and National Endowment for the Arts fellowships and is president of One Way Productions, an independent entertainment company.

Erin Khue Ninh was born in Saigon in 1973 and came to Los Angeles with her parents two years later. She is an

English major at the University of California, Berkeley. "This story," she writes, "is for my grandmother, one more thing I owe to her."

Susan Power is an enrolled member of the Standing Rock Sioux tribe (Yanktonnai Dakota) and a native Chicagoan. She received her A.B. in psychology from Harvard/ Radcliffe, J.D. from Harvard Law School, and M.F.A. from the University of Iowa Writer's Workshop. Her short fiction has been widely published in literary journals and anthologies, and she is the author of *The Grass Dancer,* a novel. She lives in Cambridge, Massachusetts.

Ruth Rambo, a.k.a. Ruth Rambo McClain, has worked in the areas of public administration, government, and community-based not-for-profit organizations for many years. Much of her experience has focused on inner-city youth. She is currently a director at the United Neighborhood Houses of New York.

Rosel Schewel grew up in Baltimore. Now retired, Ms. Schewel was a professor of education at Lynchburg College in Virginia for eighteen years. Prior to that, she was a special-education teacher in the Lynchburg public schools.

Dorothy A. Schueler is a resident of Warm Hearth Village Retirement Community in Virginia and a member of the Warm Hearth Writer's Workshop. This is her first published piece.

Ethel Morgan Smith teaches creative writing and African-American fiction at West Virginia University in Morgantown. She is a graduate of the Creative Writing Program of Hollins College and the recipient of numerous national and state grants.

Ellison Smythe, the only man in this collection, received a B.S. in electrical engineering from Virginia Polytechnic Institute in 1925, a B.D. from Union Theological Seminary in 1930, and an M.A. from Washington and Lee University in 1939. For many years Reverend Smythe served churches in West Virginia, South Carolina, and Virginia.

Nance Van Winckel is the author of *Bad Girl, with Hawk* and *The 24 Doors*. She was an NEA Fellow in 1988 and directs the writing program at Lake Forest College in Illinois.